Time continues inexorably on its path, and among
and situations that leave their marks on our live
we can distinguish a number of the points on t
found success and paved the way to forging an
and what we hold on to in the present. They are
and in our work.

What Dan Hunter proposes is irrefutable proof of this. Like the expression of his
face, his cuisine has been tempered by the years, revealing that contemporaneity
and respect for nature can come together in an attractive and relevant gastronomic
offering. His culinary creations are a compilation of the seasons, local product
cycles, and the present moment, through ideas that shake them up and set them
right again, and the weight of history and its different eras – the history of the land
he has settled – which gives his cuisine depth. The result, the sum of his experiences and times, is that Brae's offering has in only a few years earned a place
among the best restaurants in Australia, and the world. And it has done so by creating a measured and ethical style, as organic as the landscapes it represents, as
calm as the look on Dan's face, and the hillsides that give their name to his project.

Looking back, as if in a dream, invoking the past and delving into the nooks
and crannies of my time and my memories, I can still see Dan at the helm of the
kitchen at Mugaritz, with his serenity and fortitude, at the most difficult of times,
at the beginning. I honestly don't know what brought him to us, how he came to
lead us all, and why he left. But my memory recognises his being here as one of
those transcendental situations that have enabled Mugaritz to achieve what it has
achieved, and more particularly, as a way to achieve it. Today, in parallel, Mugaritz
and Brae explore the ability of local ingredients to provide us with new opportu-
nities, seeking renewed qualities and signs of the future, giving shape to new
philosophies that are in tune with the times. Techniques and products that like
words give an account of a way of existing in this world; a way of observing it;
a way of telling it as it is. Parallel paths in a reality that knows that talent and
knowledge, like challenges and problems, are global and know no borders. If we
traced an imaginary parallel that crossed both Errenteria and Birregurra, it would
reverberate with the energies that penetrate it: determination, acknowledgement
and respect. A great deal of respect, especially. Because no matter what separates
us, above everything we see what unites us: a shared memory and a cuisine inter-
twined with happiness. And this book is an example of this.

Andoni Luis Aduriz, Mugaritz

Brae

Brae
Recipes and stories
from the restaurant

Dan Hunter

Road to Brae

Road to Brae

Road to Brae

I got into cooking quite late by traditional standards, ending up in kitchens at about twenty two. And I wasn't brought up in one of those food families, in which everything revolves around family recipes. Mine was just a fairly typical Anglo-Australian upbringing that dabbled a bit with multiculturalism on the table but was probably more at ease with meat and potatoes. I enjoyed lots of sport as a kid, and food was mainly for fuel and sustenance rather than flavour or pleasure. And I didn't particularly like vegetables.

My mum is an OK cook, although she says she doesn't really like cooking. She does, however, like it when I cook and, as my siblings and I grew up, food became more important as a central theme to sharing each other's company. Of course, it's integral now.

The one thing that was always important, though, in our family, was dinnertime. No matter what was going on, it was compulsory to be at the table every night for around 6 o'clock, after sports practice or band practice, riding bikes or swimming down the river with mates – and there was absolutely no TV allowed while we were eating. I'm quite a bit older than my siblings, being the only child from my parents' marriage. They separated when I was about two and both remarried when I was six. I lived with my mum and stepdad and their three children, who are seven, nine and thirteen years younger than me.

As you can imagine with a fifteen-year-old, a two-year-old, and a couple of kids in between, dinnertime was pretty colourful and probably a bit of a bitch for whoever was cooking – this is likely the reason why my mum says she didn't enjoy it. But she still valued the act of sharing and being together and it was the only time in the day when we all had to be at the table. So, for a family who didn't seem to value the food in itself, we spent a lot of time sitting around the kitchen table.

I think those mealtimes have played a big part in shaping the kind of cook I've become and, the truth is, once I fell into cooking, it was the act of eating and sharing time at a table with friends and family that initially kept me in it. Today, with aging parents, adult siblings and partners and children all in the mix, a family gathering pretty much only ever happens at a table, where lunch usually rolls into dinner and dinner into hangovers.

Out of the city

We moved from the outer east part of Melbourne to a country town in East Gippsland, Victoria, when I was eleven years old. I couldn't believe we did that and, although Melbourne's outer east at that time was just pre-urban sprawl and still home to market gardens and paddocks, the real country felt like a cultural desert. I felt a real disconnect and probably struggled a bit with identity. I had moved a lot already as a kid but always just to another suburb or school and, given that most places we moved to were familiar, I just made new friends and got on with it. This was different. I was now in a world where kids lived on farms and rode horses and motorbikes, there was not much in the way of TV reception, and no decent music or radio stations.

I was quite good at sport and so probably used that as a tool to fit in a bit, I guess, but I never really felt like I belonged in a country town. In hindsight, I did end up having a pretty enriching time, and did plenty of things that I just wouldn't have experienced growing up surrounded by sprawling suburbia – I got a good opportunity to be outdoors and in nature but, as I got closer to finishing high school, I knew I had to get out and, at that time, I was certain I never wanted to live in a country town again.

I didn't do that well in high school. I passed the final year but didn't get into university and didn't want to go, which was a bit shitty because, for most country kids in Australia, university is at least a ticket to the city. I moved to Melbourne anyway and just tried to get into any course that would have me. I started a basic accounting/business course at a TAFE (tertiary school) and hardly ever went. I changed to another course at another school at the end of the first semester and still didn't go – this move was made in order to be in the city with friends, to be on a course to get the government study allowance (which was minimal) and to party. Jules, who was my girlfriend at that time and who is now my wife, was at uni and we just lived between each other's houses. She studied and went to school a bit during the week and I just hung out, really, going to pubs or parties or recovering.

Into a kitchen

For money, at around the age of nineteen, I got a job as a kitchen hand. I was on the dole at this stage – you could live on it at that time if your standards weren't too high. Share houses, $2 kebabs on a Tuesday, dollar pots (cheap glasses of beer), smoking weed, that type of stuff – all of it for fun. If you didn't at least pretend to apply for work, then the government cut you off, but you could also work a few hours a week without them changing your allowance too much, so it was worthwhile. I did want to do something with my life that was creative, and had a solid work ethic; but I honestly had no idea what to do. I often cursed the shitty high school teacher who convinced me (and my parents) that I should give up music as a teenager starting senior high school to concentrate on other subjects that I had no interest in and wasn't good at.

The first day I worked in a kitchen was memorable. It was upbeat, there was the feeling of being a team – something I've liked ever since about kitchens and could relate to immediately (maybe from playing team sports). And people, refreshingly, were being themselves: tatts, piercings, long-haired guys, swearing at each other and a mixed-sex environment, not just blokes. Then the other side, the dining room, was buzzing but orderly and, of course, with everyone sitting around tables, eating, drinking, talking and just enjoying themselves. I was smoking a bit of pot at this stage and definitely would have smoked before going to this job – it's what you do when you're into weed – so food and eating was definitely a priority for me. Pot smoking had certainly connected me to my sense of taste, and a job where you turn up a little bit stoned and get something good to eat seemed perfect. If people noticed they didn't seem to care too much, because it's better you washing the dishes than them.

This kitchen had a glass door that went out to the fridges and a dry store and it opened flush against the sink – it's a stupid design but typical of many restaurants that pay no attention to work flow or kitchen design in general. About three hours into my first shift, in the middle of a Friday lunch service whilst hand-washing a stack of black cast-iron pans, one slipped off the edge of the drying rack at the same time as a waiter pushed the door open and it went straight through the glass door with what is still the biggest crash I've ever heard in a restaurant. FUCK.

'What the fuck? Blah, blah, blah…' was pretty much all I remember hearing from the owner who burst in off the floor. And then the sound of glass being swept up, which is a really rough thing to hear during service. But the chef just told me not to worry, cooked me lunch and said at the end of service that although I fucked up, I still did a good job and the owner wanted me to come back if I was keen. I went back only a few more times, but this job was my first intro to a restaurant kitchen.

It was several years before I set foot in a kitchen again, and I didn't really consider that I'd be back in one – pot washing is hard physical work and my first experience in a kitchen didn't make me look at the cooks with any real envy either. I did a short government-assisted course in radio and media at a community radio station, 3CR, in Collingwood, ended up driving a delivery van for a second-hand office furniture factory in Fitzroy and then I travelled. I went to India for three months by myself on a bit of an eye-opening mission. When I returned

For money, at the age of nineteen, I got a job as a kitchen hand. I was on the dole at this stage – you could live on it at that time if your standards weren't too high.

Road to Brae

The bizarre thing was I enjoyed this work. I liked the rhythm, the energy.

I felt I had changed a lot, as you do after your first trip to a strong culture that's completely different to your own. India was cheap. I think I'd saved $3,000 and it got me a return flight and three months travel, food and accommodation. But I did it real rough, staying in basically the cheapest accommodation I could find and eating vegetarian basics.

When I got back, Jules had planned a trip through East Africa with a close friend, with Europe as their final destination. They weren't leaving for a couple of months and I thought I'd be able to work a few jobs and save enough money to go with them. I decided I'd need two jobs to do this. Given I had no qualifications in anything, any job was inevitably going to be labour based and lowly paid. I got a job assembling light fittings with a small Italian company in Carlton. But at least it was full time, Monday to Friday. We started early and were finished by 4.00 p.m. I lived in North Melbourne at the time, and rode my bike to and from work so as not to spend money on trams. After a few months of this, I could see I needed another income to have any chance of saving the money I needed to at least get a ticket abroad. I applied for a job as a kitchen hand in a pub in Ascot Vale and started doing three to four nights a week there. After finishing the eight-hour shift assembling lights, I would ride home, have something to eat, then ride to the pub to start my shift at 5.30 p.m. and work 'till closing time.

Now, this job was a bitch. It was a busy pub and I don't think they really did any dishes or pot washing throughout the day before I started. There would be lots of plates waiting and also a mound of pots and pans circling the sink and spreading onto the floor. It would take a couple of hours just to get rid of the lunch dishes and then the dinner ones would start arriving. The stock pots were so big I had to lay them on their sides on the floor and crawl into them to scrub the bottoms. And inevitably, like in lots of shitty places that have little respect for the kitchen hands, there would be heaps of pots that were badly burnt and tucked in amongst the rest like a nasty surprise.

The bizarre thing was I enjoyed this work. I liked the rhythm, the energy, the waves of increased pressure and workload, the shit-stirring between the chefs and, inevitably, between me and the chefs, the rush and the clean down, the laughs, the calm and then, the next day, doing it all again. Maybe I enjoyed it as I could see the endgame: work like a bastard and then go away and travel.

After a few months of this routine (lights during the day, talking shit with Italian guys and drinking lots of espressos, then scrubbing burnt cheese off pizza trays from badly cooked chicken parmas at night), I realised I wasn't getting close to having enough money to leave at the same time as Jules, so I resigned myself to the fact that this would be my life for a little while. I thought I would move out of Melbourne and answered a job ad in the paper for a kitchen hand in a little restaurant on the Great Ocean Road in Apollo Bay. It mentioned doing some basic food prep and I had been doing a little bit of putting some desserts onto plates at the pub – so the chefs could leave early – so when I spoke to the chef over the phone I said I could do some basics and he gave me the job right then on the spot.

Within a week or so we had moved out of our house and I moved down to Apollo Bay. I stayed at a backpackers' hostel for a bit while I settled in and found a house. I did as many hours as I could washing dishes. The food prep turned out to be washing leaves, peeling vegetables and making sandwiches for the staff, frying the odd basket of chips and putting fruit purées into bottles.

This was towards the end of summer, before the Easter rush. I was getting lots of hours, and working at a small restaurant felt like a step up from pot scrubbing at a pub. The people there were mostly casual workers and international travellers doing a summer job, but the restaurant was owned by a family who had run it for years and, as simple as the food was, they were passionate about doing things well.

I stayed in Apollo Bay until after Easter when things started to die down and I had saved enough money to get myself to Europe, with a bit of cash to last a month or so. I wasn't sure what I would do in Europe after meeting up with Jules but music festivals and dance parties were high on the agenda.

13

Road to Brae

Jules and I met up in Amsterdam. She had been in London for a week or so before I got there and she came across to meet me. We had a week there before going to London. I had some friends there who I'd met in India and, after staying at a backpackers' place briefly, they gave us a place to stay for a couple of nights.

Glastonbury festival was a day or two away and we had decided to go and jump the fence, catching a bus from London via Bath. Bath had been a topic of conversation while we were staying in London. We needed to work and save money so we could get to Central America. Our plan was to travel through Guatemala, Honduras and Mexico for six months. So we needed to be somewhere that didn't suck money like London can. Our friends suggested Bath and we thought we might check it out after the festival.

Glastonbury was big. We jumped off the bus in the crawling traffic, scaled the walls, got in, paid a tenner to a bouncer from Bristol and stayed for the entire festival. It was one of those wet years with mud up to your knees most of the time and, if you weren't careful you ended up waist-deep or lying fully submerged. Pretty fucking disgusting really but a real party – 120,000 people going for it.

After the final day we were exhausted, still wearing garbage bags to try to keep the mud at bay and were on the bus back to London, via Bath. I think we'd forgotten about the conversation we'd had the week before about Bath but when we pulled into the bus stop and couldn't really take being covered in mud any more, we decided to get off and spend a couple of nights there.

We stayed at the YMCA for a few nights and, on the first or second night, I saw a job ad on their noticeboard for a chef at a local pub. I called the number and arranged an interview for the following day. It was at a pub a little out of town, run by a Welsh couple who were friendly enough, but there were certainly a few miserable bastards working there. The couple picked me up for the interview and said they could provide transport to and from the centre of Bath each working day, even between the split shifts. I thought at the time that they must have been a bit desperate and soon found out that was true as, following the interview and a bit of embellishment of my cooking background and skills, I got the job as a chef.

So, having had four or five months of washing dishes and occasionally putting a few strawberries and cream on a plate while one of the actual chefs had a ciggy or went home, I now had a paid a job in a foreign country as a chef. No knives, no whites, and no real cooking skills apart from what I cooked at home. I realised I was probably in a bit of trouble but chose not to pay much attention to this fact. I hadn't gone too crazy in the interview and did say that I was travelling and only wanted to work for six months or so, I'd only done very basic cold prep, but still I could see that they'd probably want a bit more from me. After the interview, I picked up Jules and went straight to the Bath library to do a real quick apprenticeship. I 'borrowed' three books that day that I still have, and that got me through the five months I ended up staying at the pub: *The Joy of Cooking*, *Sophie Grigson's Meat Course* and *Leith's Cookery School*.

Now this place was special. It was called The Blathwayt Arms. In the kitchen there was Rob, the publican, who was basically giving up cooking, and Andy, a northerner who was miserable and really the guy in charge of the kitchen. Andy shared this information at every opportunity with not only Rob and the other staff but random customers who would catch him as he him came down from his room upstairs on his way to the kitchen. Then there was John, or Crazy John, who was completely paranoid from smoking weed and who smoked weed at the kitchen door continually throughout the day, and Clive, a kitchen hand who dressed in a kilt, did his face like Alice Cooper, and would drink a gallon of cider on the break in the afternoon before returning to work.

I cut my teeth in this shop

After a few weeks of doing basic veg prep and whatever else had to be done, pretty much in the role of a commis, I was pushed up a bit. Rob no longer worked

I felt like I had gone away to travel and party, and had inadvertently made an important decision about what I wanted to do.

in the kitchen very often and Andy did fuck all. John worked when he could cope, although every time did, he screamed 'fuckin' wankers' into the dining room during service and smashed a ladle into the bain-marie; he and Rob nearly came to blows. I was trying to understand as much as I could from the three books I had – trying to work things out like what 'braising' meant, why you would seal meat before stewing it, why potatoes went gluey if mashed at the wrong temperature, and trying to put some order into the cool room at a place where no-one really cared what they served or how they left the kitchen. Still, I was into it and I was starting to cook a few things for the menu – an adaptation of the dry chicken curry from *Sophie Grigson's Meat Course* was an early signature.

After roughly five months I left the Blathwayt and did a few shifts at a little restaurant in the city of Bath. Jules and I had saved enough money to get to Central America and were pretty pleased to be going. We had been living in a terrible, damp house, it was winter and, really, after working in that pub with those guys, I was pretty ready for a change.

Central America was another eye-opener. The thing that still stands out is the memory of travelling somewhere where food was central to the culture. I flipped out in Mexico particularly, and was eating as much as possible. Those few months in a kitchen as a cook had created an interest in food that I never had before and I spent a big portion of that trip tasting as many new things as I could.

For me, it was the first time I could see the important relationship between food and a country's DNA. Jules's family is Italian and she grew up surrounded by food. On festive days throughout the year, her family prepared, cooked and ate special things together. Even though we had been together for a few years by then, it was really during this trip that I started to understand what that all meant in Jules's life. I started thinking on this trip that maybe cooking and restaurants was something I would look into a bit more seriously.

After our trip we returned to the UK, this time to London. We needed to work to get a ticket home. I ended up at an agency doing casual work at a few places but mainly at a nursing home in Kensington. Sandwiches, purées, salads and cutting fruit – all the big stuff.

I could actually cook a few things by now and was developing a little bit of a palate – understanding how much salt to put in and when it should be added, things like that. For about five or six months I worked at this home and, for the last few months, I cooked the evening meal for the forty or so residents. Now, this was in Kensington and it was a high-end nursing home, so they ate pretty well. The only thing was that a lot of the guests were beyond cutting and chewing so, each day, I carefully designed a three-course meal with the main always containing meat and accompanying vegetables, cooked in various ways, and then puréed the lot into three different-coloured blobs. Many people have commented throughout my career on how well I can make a purée.

I was pretty certain now that when we got back to Melbourne after this trip, I would start an apprenticeship in a kitchen. I felt like I had gone away to travel and party and had inadvertently made an important decision about what I wanted to do. I didn't know anyone who worked in restaurants but I had decided, after seeing all the terrible kitchens and food cooked badly by people who hated their jobs and didn't care about the customers, that I wanted to see another, better side of cooking, where skills were valued and respect for the job at hand was second nature. Once we settled back into Melbourne life, I started applying for work as a first-year apprentice. It was January 1999 and I was twenty four.

Kitchens in Melbourne

All through this formative time in my career I was lucky to have good mentors, who had similar values and who were tradespeople with a strong grasp of technique.

I started my apprenticeship in a seafood restaurant, the Melbourne Oyster Bar, under Adrian Upward, a chef, to whom I'm very grateful. At twenty four, I only had pot-washing skills and probably some bad cooking habits picked up

Road to Brae

in pretty average kitchens. Adrian helped me onto a good path. I think I was probably a bit of a novelty, being a twenty-four-year-old first-year rather than the typical sixteen-to-seventeen-year-old, but feeling as though I had lots to learn to catch up with others my age meant I really put my head down. I went to trade school and was lucky to be awarded some financial scholarships, which helped, as that first year I remember earning just over $200 a week.

After eighteen months there, and a few beers after work one night, the chef mentioned to me that he thought I'd grown out of the type of restaurant that the oyster bar was, and that putting up hundreds of seafood platters each week was probably a bit limiting for my development. He said he would sort me out. At the time, a restaurant called Langton's was considered among Melbourne's best. He phoned the chef there, Philippe Mouchel, on my behalf, and asked if they needed anyone in the kitchen. That call got me a trial.

Langton's was the first real kitchen I had been in. Philippe Mouchel had previously run the Paul Bocuse restaurant in Tokyo and had opened Bocuse's restaurant in Melbourne. When I went for my trial, there were probably fifteen chefs working, and the restaurant was full at lunch and booked out for dinner – I was pretty overwhelmed but remember thinking that this was more like it. A restaurant with career chefs and skilled service staff. A serious head chef with plenty of cred, backed up by a solid army. And actual technical preparations and cooking – wall-mounted rotisserie, butchers trimming meat, pastry chefs speaking French – all the clichés, but at the time pretty exciting.

I got that job and started the following week. About a week later, Philippe resigned, giving a couple of months' notice and, through the panic of feeling as though they were not going to get his food anymore, the Melbourne dining public went mental and booked out the restaurant every day till he left. Basically 100-plus for lunch and 100-plus for dinner every day – I had never worked so hard.

I had eaten one really great meal in Melbourne that year, at a restaurant called Pomme, owned by Jeremy Strode. It was with Jules for my birthday, and it was probably the best restaurant meal I had eaten at that stage: super-seasonal, beautifully presented and really quite simple – just a few things on each plate. I had a lobster entrée, lamb and aubergine (eggplant) and then a grapefruit 'delicious'. I can still remember it quite vividly, right down to the Turkish delight petit four. At the time I thought that it was the sort of food I'd like to cook. Pomme was a chef's restaurant – it had the highest rating in the local food guide, small numbers and lovely service, led by Jeremy's business partner Chris Young, who ran the front of house. I don't know if Melbourne wasn't ready for a restaurant like that, or it was just in the wrong part of the city, but Pomme went under and soon closed down. The only benefit to me was that Jeremy took over from Philippe at Langton's and was my chef for the next two years.

I learnt a lot in my years working for Jeremy. I did every section and spent a long time on both the fish and the meat and sauce sections. Jeremy spent a lot of time with me, and I made sure I did whatever was needed. If you are going to become comfortable in restaurant kitchens at a certain level, I think you need to spend solid time with someone just doing what you're told while always pushing yourself to discover nuances within the techniques you are learning and to continually improve. I don't think it's very beneficial to move around a lot in the first few years that you work in demanding kitchens. You need time to have an initial freak-out and then find your feet and enjoy cooking with the confidencethat comes from that, while still being in an environment where your only responsibilities are within your section.

One thing that became clear while working at a restaurant like Langton's, and under a chef like Jeremy, was that I needed to work somewhere other than Australia to really see what was going on in a strong international restaurant. I wanted to see if I was up to it. At that time in Melbourne there was a fairly large contingent of French-trained, English chefs running kitchens and, in a way, dictating the style of cuisine within many of the top kitchens. The food media referred to them as the

The thing that stands out still, is the memory of travelling somewhere where food was central to the culture. I flipped out in Mexico particularly, and was eating as much as possible.

'Brit Pack' – and a lot of what was going on in London kitchens was transported to Melbourne, in a slightly more casual way. A lot of Australians were training under these guys and then, under the working holiday visa arrangement, they would go to London, walk into the kitchens that their chefs had come from and complete the circle once they returned. To be honest, I thought that period of time in Melbourne was boring. For my palate at least, the food was too rich, full of too much butter and cream, lacking in precision and in a sense, as everyone seemed to be cooking the same things, it felt mainstream. Jeremy was a little different. He was more focused on a lighter cuisine and vegetables, delivered with an equal lightness of touch.

I didn't see the point of being another Aussie chef in an Aussie kitchen in London. Along with many interests I had at the time, I felt like I wanted to do something different. After a couple of years under and then alongside him, Jeremy, like my first chef Adrian, encouraged me to think about moving on to something more challenging. In his kitchen in that first year, the sous chef, Joe, had just returned from working in Italy at Gualtiero Marchesi's three-star restaurant. He was in my ear from the start to get out of Melbourne and see a different cooking culture – France or Italy, knowing that Jules was Italian – and also talked on and off about the new wave of cooking coming out of Spain.

This was the early 2000s, when the news of Ferran Adrià broke to the rest of the world. Joe showed me Italian magazines, beautiful professional food publications, of a quality that I had never seen before in Australia and that probably didn't exist in the English language at that time. I remember a picture of a dish of some type of consommé noodles – it looked incredible and immediately piqued my interest, and was a lot more exciting than frothed fish veloutés on fish mousses, which was how the English-speaking world seemed to be cooking.

I started honing in on the idea of working in Europe. Jules and I had learnt some Spanish while travelling in Central America and had flirted with the idea of Spain. We certainly wanted to live in Europe and have the chance to learn more languages.

I finished at Langton's and took a position in the kitchen at another Melbourne restaurant called Verge. I was feeling like I needed a change of pace and accepted a chef de partie role (in charge of one area of production in the kitchen), just working Monday to Friday, and starting early, a couple of hours before anyone else. I was responsible for all the stocks, sauces and butchery, and for coming up with menu items and a couple of specials each day. I had never had the chance just to be in a kitchen alone before, watching things cook, taking my time, with no one on my back, deciding to do things in a manner that I thought was right, not just following direction. This actually turned out to be a pivotal time in my career – it was the first real opportunity I had to work on the creative side of cooking while actually having the time, alone, to work on skills.

While working at Verge I came across a publication called *Spain Gourmet Tour*, published by the economic and commercial development arm of the Spanish government. This magazine focused on Spanish food culture, was written in English and I guess it was used as a tool to promote tourism. I was fascinated by it. Not long after starting at Verge, Jules and I made the decision to attempt to live and work in Spain. She has an Italian passport and, after we were married, I was able to obtain European residency for five years. I stayed at Verge for twelve months, and was reading as much as possible about different cuisines and chefs in Spain. Of course, elBulli and Ferran were central to nearly every article. From the outside, elBulli seemed like the biggest group of punks to ever cook – they seemed to be taking every preconception and turning it upside down, and I loved that there seemed to be absolutely no reference whatsoever to the English-speaking world or anything that might be going on in the British or French kitchens that everyone in Melbourne was still making reference to.

A few months before we left Australia, an article appeared in *Spain Gourmet Tour* about some upcoming chefs making names for themselves at that time. I still didn't know where I wanted to work in Spain – at that point, the plan consisted of

Road to Brae

no more than this: get to Barcelona, try to learn some of the language and have a bit of a party. So far, most of the information available in English about Spanish chefs had focused on Ferran, but this article featured others who had great restaurants and are still around today. The one guy I can vividly remember sticking out, for the intensity of his gaze, and for the very clear and precise use of language to describe the type of natural cuisine he was cooking, was Andoni Luis Aduriz. Off the back of that article I decided I would try to work at his restaurant Mugaritz. I really had no idea how that was going to happen but it became part of the plan.

Spain

After spending a couple of months in Barcelona, and a few failed and somewhat embarrassing job interviews in very broken Spanish, I got a position with the Ritz Hotel at their signature restaurant, Diana. Although the kitchen was quite French (bizarrely for Barcelona), the pastry chef spoke perfect English and needed a commis. I was told if I could start immediately I'd have a job. Leading up to that, I'd sent or dropped off a resume and covering letter to every restaurant in Barcelona with a Michelin star. I heard back from maybe two or three but was really struggling with the language and starting to get a bit worried that I might never get a job. I had been quite naïve, in a way, to think I would ever get into a decent kitchen in Spain with no contacts and no language.

Anyway, Diana wasn't really where I wanted to be, cooking essentially French food with a Catalan accent. The chef there had worked for Alain Ducasse and a lot of that experience was ingrained in the bones of the kitchen. I had chosen Spain with the intention of cooking a cuisine I could not cook anywhere else and had instead ended up cooking the same style of food that I found boring in London and Melbourne. After about six months, the restaurant closed for a big refurbishment: a new kitchen, redesigned dining room, all the bells and whistles, plus a new name, Caelis. It seemed to gain a star for investment alone! And, overall, I was happy enough to have the opportunity to be in a kitchen learning some Spanish, with the chance to communicate in English as a fall back.

While I was in Barcelona, the word about Andoni and Mugaritz was growing throughout Spain and I was becoming more convinced that it was ridiculous to stay in Barcelona and cook French food. The restaurant elBulli was still on everyone's lips, but within Spain at the time, and particularly in Barcelona, strangely this style of food and the restaurant itself was almost becoming mainstream. Mugaritz seemed to be more cutting edge. The Basques are always looked down on a little by the rest of Spain for being freaks: no one knows where they came from and it seems as if they're still misunderstood. I made contact with Mugaritz to enquire about a position starting in 2005 and was told I could come and do a three-month stage but with no promise of any employment at the end of it. Jules and I decided that we would move to Donosti at that time. In August, when most of central and southern Spain closes down for the annual summer vacations, Jules and I went on a trip across the entire northern coast of Spain, starting in Donosti and ending in Galicia. We went for four weeks but spent one full week in Donosti to get a feel for it, to check out where we might live and, of course, to eat at Mugaritz. I remember we ate at lunchtime. The restaurant was half empty and it rained, hard summer rain, for about three hours. During that time we agreed that this was the best restaurant meal we had ever eaten, and secondly, that I had to work at this restaurant.

Mugaritz

We arrived in Spain in early 2003 and I began my position as a stagiaire at Mugaritz in January 2005. After this stage period, I finished without an official offer of employment but was contacted a week or so later and asked if I wanted to start as a chef de partie, an offer I accepted. At the beginning of 2006, I was made a sous chef and then, shortly after, I moved into the chef de cuisine position when the person in that job left the business. I stayed in that role until the end of 2006.

If we're open to change and discovery, we look forward rather than back and are comfortable with the concept of being in constant evolution.

How do you measure the impact or result of important life events? Surely, most of us are merely the sum of the lives we've lived to date. Of course, if we're open to change and discovery, look forward rather than back and are comfortable with the concept of being in constant evolution, the smallest, most insignificant moments or decisions can have major implications on our life paths. For some, the exposure over time to certain people and their ideas can make you reset your views. This can be positive, but also negative for people who are easily swayed and quick to claim the views of others. It's possible to encounter people from completely different cultures and backgrounds and discover an unexpected like-mindedness. To find views that you consider to be aligned with your own, even though you may not ever have shared a common path, to discover a similar work ethic and commitment, to agree to view certain things as serious but always with an eye on humour, to feel challenged but respected, and to be pushed but encouraged and to work with acute discipline, but be free.

I've always found it a little difficult to summarise what it was like to work at Mugaritz and what I took away from the experience. It's certainly not a place where I learnt to cook the basics, and I think I've learnt far more about cooking in the last decade of making my own food than in all the time I spent cooking the food of others. Having said that, it's a place that really opened my eyes to the possibilities of what restaurants can be. At that stage I had never seen so much thought go into not only cooking but also into the relationships the restaurant had with the environment and suppliers: the research, selection and storage of raw ingredients; the detail in the dining room; and the management and curation of the dining experience, from the time a guest makes a booking through to their departure.

Seeing how things were done at Mugaritz made me realise that you could be actively anti-establishment, but be passive. And I also realised that a restaurant being anti-establishment could be a positive thing, that it's possible to make noise whilst working in silence, and that being away from the noise of others could allow focus and continual consideration and refinement of your own values, which is important when crafting experiences with identity. I didn't learn to cook at Mugaritz, but being there helped me develop the skills and confidence to decide how and what I want to cook.

Returning home

When we returned to Australia after living in Spain for close to four years, the initial plan was to move back to Melbourne and work for someone. This was 2007 and still, at that stage, owning a restaurant was not on the agenda. I thought I could come back and get a job running a kitchen for someone who would be on the same wavelength, who would be interested in doing something special, and that they'd give me enough creative freedom to make the venue successful. Melbourne was where we had lived for over ten years before going to Spain and, during difficult times in Spain, Melbourne was often the place we wanted to be. In our minds we probably painted too perfect a picture of Melbourne, but we soon realised that, in the time we had been away, quite a bit had changed. Finding a house to rent was a bitch, there seemed to be a lot more motor traffic in the inner city and, from a professional point of view, after working so closely with small producers within a food-rich culture like the Basque region, a lot of what I saw in the marketplace, particularly vegetable-wise, seemed pretty substandard.

Unfortunately, too, after being back for a few months and a couple of positions ending up being dead ends with no visible potential for improvement, I found myself unemployed and what felt like unemployable. I had no money to start even approaching investors — I had been in Spain for nearly four years, just scraping by. And, in a way, because what was happening in Spain was still largely unknown in Australia, it was like I was an unknown entity. Mugaritz had just appeared in the top ten of the San Pellegrino World's 50 Best list but, at that point, the list didn't have the relevance it does today. Because at that stage there was no English spoken at Mugaritz, not many journalists from the English-speaking world, particularly

Road to Brae

Australia, bothered to write anything about the restaurant. There had been one article written in *Gourmet Traveller* magazine about the fact that I was the head chef there, but really not many Australians had even eaten there back then.

I left a job I was trying hard to make good in, even though I could sense it was going nowhere, and had a bit of a meltdown. We had left Spain just as I was starting to get the hang of running a kitchen at that level in a foreign language because we were basically broke and homesick and now, at this point, I remember feeling a bit the same – but in reverse.

The road finding us

There was an article in the Melbourne food press, 'Epicure', in *The Age* newspaper, covering the fact that I was a free agent, and that same morning I answered a call from someone I'd never heard of, talking about a small hotel I had never heard of, in a town that was around three-and-a-half hours' drive from Melbourne, that I'd also never heard of. It was called the Royal Mail Hotel in Dunkeld. I remember holding the phone away from my ear, as I thought that whatever was being described to me was the last thing I wanted to do at this stage. I had imagined a typical home-coming success story on my return. In this scenario, I'd walk straight into the perfect city restaurant, backed by lots of money and with full creative control, cooking for a receptive audience and then, basically, conquer the world – yeah right! Instead, there I was, unemployed three months after getting back, listening to a story about a pub from a total stranger. I arranged to hear more of this story face to face in a bar that Friday night and, after not really paying attention to anything that was said, I met with Jules and explained that we'd been invited to this place the following week to have a look. In all honesty, the only thing we thought was that at least it would be a night away with accommodation and a meal thrown in and, given that we literally had nothing better to do, what was there to lose?

After a twenty-four-hour interview and walk around the town and properties, it was arranged that I'd get back to these guys if I was interested. The hotel was neither in the city nor established as a destination in its own right. There appeared to be plenty of the correct sentiment behind the business to make something work and, certainly, there was infrastructure in terms of land, equipment and labour to produce the food required by a gastronomic restaurant. I took a month to decide. It really came out of the blue and was not in any way what I imagined I'd be doing upon returning to Australia, but in the end, we decided, just like with the initial meeting, that given there was nothing better to do and that we could always leave if things weren't right, to take a leap, again into the unknown – and I took the job. At the same time Jules took a job there as marketing manager.

I stayed in that position for six years. The restaurant won much acclaim and I built a reputation that helped me to make the next move, but a couple of years in, I knew that being so far from the city and a dining population, in general, wasn't for me. I also realised that I had a very clear vision for what I wanted a restaurant to be and, unfortunately, I was in the wrong place. We started looking for a site after two years of working at the hotel, and it took almost four years to find somewhere that fit the necessary requirements of the restaurant we had now decided we wanted to own and work in.

We had decided as a rough starting point that the place had to be within 150 kilometres of Melbourne, surrounded by rich agricultural land with mixed farming and good rainfall, it had to have a good density of population or good roads and transport to get people there, be close to the coast, close to a town but not in it, and on a small property with enough land to grow food, but not too much land that looking after it becomes a burden. Four years! Four years of sitting tight, of travelling around the state looking at every venue that could somehow meet the requirements, of doing budgets and trying to convince ourselves that options that were obviously wrong could work, of trying just to keep our eye on what could be, all whilst maintaining and improving standards and a reputation so that, when it happened, there would be something the public would come for.

In August 2013, with the help of business partners, we finally purchased a thirty-acre property located 135 kilometres south west of Melbourne, on the edge of the town of Birregurra, in the Otways hinterland. Named Sunnybrae, it was, for a long time, a restaurant and cooking school, based in an old red-brick cottage. Built in the 1860s by Scottish settlers who farmed potatoes, oats, pigs and cattle amongst other things, it also had a weatherboard extension tacked onto the back in the 1980s that housed a commercial kitchen and three small rooms that acted as a dining space. To my eye, the property was beautiful but tired and in need of some love, and for our needs, the existing building that housed the restaurant needed significant renovation, but there was definite potential. Everything else met our criteria – under 150 kilometres from Melbourne, a good parcel of land with some existing fruit trees and vegetable gardens treated organically, a small olive grove, plenty of water from four dams around the property, and plenty of space to increase food production and potentially build some accommodation. The Otways are renowned for good annual rainfall and there is an abundance of mixed agricultural activity close by, from dairy farming to berry production. The ocean is close, with the Great Ocean Road under half an hour's drive away – Geelong, Victoria's second city after Melbourne, is around 40 minutes away and both of Melbourne's airports are west of the city centre, making it easy for international and interstate visitors to reach us. There was plenty of work to do to get the property to anywhere near a level that would really satisfy the idea that existed in my mind, but more than any other place and property we'd seen previously, it felt right.

In December that year, four months after taking over the property and completing a major renovation of the existing building and grounds, we opened Brae.

The Restaurant

The Restaurant

The Restaurant

The Restaurant

Brae \\'brā\ *n.* — A hillside; a gentle slope.
A modern restaurant set on thirty productive acres. A place to interact with nature and eat from the land.

I want Brae to be an immersive experience. Yes, we are a restaurant and the core of what we do will always be serving food and drinks to our guests, but for a long time, while working for others, and then with all the planning that goes into opening a restaurant, I wanted to somehow offer more. I wanted our guests to pass through the front gate and immediately feel something: to drive up the driveway and be at ease; to notice the care that goes into the surrounding land and gardens and enjoy the results; to feel welcomed and cared for by our family; to find not only nourishment in the food but also in the gesture of hospitality; and for the entire experience to resonate with the same voice – cohesively, across the board.

There's a history to this property, and although I don't want the restaurant to necessarily carry the values and weight of another time, I do want us to work towards and within the somewhat idyllic values and possibilities of what a generous country house and property can mean. I've spent a good amount of time in rural Australia, and also in the homes of farming families in many other parts of the world. If you could take a mix of the best parts of those experiences you could create a kind of productive restaurant utopia – a place where you go to eat and drink abundantly from the land and nearby sea, including drinking pure rain water and being close to a wood fire on which meats and vegetables are roasting, and bread is cooking, where the food is refined in terms of the commitment and skill put into producing it, but the flavours can be rustic, grounded and more flavoursome than you've experienced, and you're in the company of the people who work that land (not just the cooking, but also the planning, planting and harvesting) and prepare that food from scratch, and everything is considered, from your comfort to the music, and all that's there is yours if you want it. And that's it really, the thing we aim for at Brae – the spirit of that feeling, of being in that place. I hope that, somehow, we can convey those feelings and values in this farmhouse.

I love it that when you sit in the dining room at Brae, your outlook is across the land, across fruit trees and olives, with chooks, bees and veggies in sight, and you become aware of the fact that people work and care for that land, and of something real and wholesome. I think it's important to understand how food is made, how it appears on our tables, and the importance of the efforts of those who grow and produce our food. But having said that, I don't think restaurants are a place for preaching – a bit of dialogue here and there is fine, but they should be for enjoyment and a little bit of hedonism. And so we made a decision not to preach to our guests about food provenance, but it's there in plain sight. You sit amongst it; it's visible. There is, hopefully, a transparency to what we do, an honesty – like the work of farmers or people involved in honing a craft. The kitchen is open and visible, the restaurant is light and surrounded by windows. You drive by an orchard and garden upon entry. Of course, we buy and serve many things that we don't grow or farm ourselves, and we're lucky that most of what we need can be found in the region we work and live in, but I personally don't see the need to lecture guests while they're at our table. We run the property in a responsible way that's healthy for the land and for those eating the food. Surely, everyone who actually cares for land and for people would grow food in the same way, if given a choice. We don't talk down to guests like we know something they don't, but we do want to share a dialogue about ethics and honesty, as well as flavour and the value of hospitality, so rather than do it verbally, we do it with the way in which we work, and we're there with them and they sit right in the middle of it all. Hopefully, this visual dialogue extends to something greater than just the meal.

There's lots of talk of time and place when discussing food and it's not just a trend for restaurants. Time, place, locally grown and indigenous ingredients are the basis of all regional cuisines and they are major influences on the cuisine at Brae. I'm Australian, and Brae is undoubtedly an Australian restaurant. We live and work in a region of southeastern Australia, growing and buying food that exists and thrives in this part of the world. I'm fortunate to live in a multicultural country, to have travelled and lived internationally and to be informed by an open, free-moving society that picks and chooses from everywhere. With all of that freedom and cherry picking, though, it still seems appropriate to me to live and work within our geographical means, to spend time getting to know and understanding the climate and environment we live in, and to focus on what's growing in the wild, and what can grow well in our paddocks and those of our neighbours. But our aim is to take all of this and present it in a way that's hopefully not considered traditional, so that there's another layer to the experience, a layer of surprise and authenticity. We want to provide our guests with an experience that, on any given day, can only be had at Brae, one that reflects the moment, our weather, our seasons and our ability to synthesize all of that into a meal, so our guests can be in that moment too.

The Food

The Food

The Food

<u>The concept</u>

Each day, the highest-quality ingredients are carefully selected from Brae's on-site organic fruit and vegetable garden, local farms and ethical, sustainable producers from Victoria and beyond. Then, treated with the greatest respect, these ingredients are transformed into the day's menu.

In the planning stages for Brae, when I was considering all the details regarding our identity and the type of experience I wanted our guests to have and take away with them, I decided that the food we serve should always reflect who we are at the present time, that it should continually evolve and be mostly made up of humble home-grown, locally grown or wild ingredients that mirror the season, the current day's weather and our geographical region.

On top of that, I found myself reflecting on the significance of the fact that we operate within a renovated farmhouse that appears, from the outside, as if it could be someone's home. The farmhouse and family home themes are ones that keep popping up for me at Brae, as is the idea of a family business situated on a small property, serving the food it produces. Yes, of course it's a restaurant and a commercial space. The bad version of that, particularly in a creative space like ours where the offering is a tasting menu, is that the guest-server relationship can be cold, with the staff seeming mechanical, cooks and servers going through the same motions service after service. Essentially, when guests come to Brae, we try to welcome them as if they are coming into our home. Of course, most guests make reservations rather than being personally invited, but internally, with Jules and myself and with our team, we make a point of trying to deal with our guests in a way that is warm and welcoming and, as much as possible, as though they are friends who have been invited over.

If you come to my house, say, for lunch, most often it will go something like this: we start with a few bits and pieces to share and nibble on while we say hello and drink some beers, cocktails or champagne. We will probably stand around the kitchen or, on a nice day, we'll be outside. I'll probably be getting on with a fire, raising it to the right temperature for roasting or barbecuing meat, and finishing off some vegetable prep along the way. After an hour or so, once we're all there, having finished picking at whatever snacks we started with – probably some cured meats or fish, a fresh cheese, maybe some pickled vegetables – and finished our drinks, we'll probably all move to a table and then start with some vegetable dishes, raw things from the garden prepared and dressed simply, good bread and butter from the restaurant, some fish or shellfish cooked over the coals. We'll share these from dishes placed between us. I'll get a piece of meat roasting slowly and keep an eye on it while we eat the first round at the table and, after a while, when we've finished, the meat will be rested and ready to go. Whatever piece of meat we eat will be carved and placed on platters to share and probably one or two simple vegetable preparations will be put alongside. We're drinking all the time and there's a genuine feeling of sharing and informality and, each time we change food, wines are poured. Some cheese, but not always, might follow before we take a break to stretch our legs outside. Dessert will be fruit-based and not super-sweet, before a coffee and something to finish, like a biscuit or small chocolate. Some beers or digestives may take us into the night.

The menu at Brae is, hopefully, reflective of what we would eat if we ate together informally. I thought a lot about how I like to eat when I invite friends or family over and have tried to base the menu around that. Yes, it's a tasting menu but, in a way, even though at home we may eat from a shared plate, we do seem to eat quite focused dishes of just a couple of ingredients at their peak, and the meal is often broken up into stages.

The Brae menu is obviously more focused than what I would generally cook at home, but in essence, like a lot of things we do at Brae, we try to at least capture the spirit of a meal you may eat at the home of friends – something generous, delicious, with obvious gestures of effort. And it is seasonal, with a strong emphasis on our own home-grown produce.

The menu

We hope that your interest is engaged as soon as you enter the property, and that the momentum of this interest continues to flow when you are presented with our menu, which is designed to bring you the best of what we have to offer. Our intention is for you to feel as though you are in for a treat, something special, from the very start of the meal to the end.

The menu is separated into four parts but can probably be summed up by two categories – things you eat with your hands and things eaten with cutlery.

A welcome, some snacks and bites

We start with some small things, to be eaten with the hands in one or two bites, a mix of dishes based on the season or the day, to pick at and share while you're enjoying champagne. We have simple offerings, such as a perfect asparagus spear, picked just before service and treated with the utmost care – peeled with a knife rather than hacked to death with a peeler, then simply blanched and rolled in butter infused with sea lettuce. Some of our bites are more thought out, tested and technical, like the iced oyster, the tiny raw peas with lemon aspen in a tart, or trout roe with crushed pistachios covered in borage flowers.

I try to encourage a feeling at this stage that it won't be too formal an experience, and find that eating with the hands is a great way to set the tone – it's relaxed and you can make a mess and eat as you would if you were at the home of a friend. Our aim is to offer the chance to eat things in their purest form – and just a bite – bits and pieces intensely focused, so there can be no mistake in terms of flavour and, hopefully, one of the best versions of that thing you've ever eaten, or maybe a new food experience altogether.

This part of the menu – a little barrage of seven to ten mini-dishes – offered before we serve you any bread and butter, is our way of the kitchen saying, 'Welcome to Brae, we've spent all morning getting this ready for you and we want you to enjoy yourselves. We're going to do all we can to make your experience with us special'. I hope this section of the menu feels like an opening act, before we settle into the nitty-gritty. You get to meet some of the main characters of the season here, but some of the more complex storylines lie ahead in the coming acts.

Knives, forks, spoons, plates

This part of the menu comprises the bulk of what we serve. We like to give both our savoury and sweet dishes an individual focus, giving each course the attention it deserves without one being unnecessarily larger. This is when you sit down to savour and appreciate a variety of flavours and textures, and we would hope to sustain your engagement with interesting combinations that taste surprisingly natural. We tend to begin lightly with delicate, subtle flavours, and progress to more instensely flavoured dishes.

The sweet part of the meal will usually consist of a couple of dishes and is often eaten after a walk in the garden or out by the bread oven and chargrill, allowing guests to walk around the property and get a feel for the surrounding environment and current season, and to see the source of much of the food they have just eaten.

Finally, following dessert, we like to offer a small bite that can be eaten with or without a herbal infusion from the garden, such as Black Mitcham or Moroccan mint blended with river mint, a native Australian herb, or a fruitier, more acidic style of coffee brewed through a filter, that to me, seems more appropriate after a menu such as ours, rather than a milk-based coffee or a harsh, dark-roast espresso.

43

Brae Gardens

46   Brae Gardens

Brae Gardens

Restaurant-kitchen gardens

For a long time now I've been convinced of the many benefits of a kitchen and restaurant working closely with its own organic vegetable and fruit garden, and one of my reasons for wanting to operate a restaurant on a property with ample space to grow food was to continue to develop this logical co-existence.

I'm a firm believer that fruits and vegetables taste better when they are grown organically and are consumed soon after being harvested. The depth of flavour found in root vegetables, the freshness and intensity of stem and leaf plants, or the diversity of produce available that, when left to ripen correctly, could not make it to market or survive the transport and storage periods of traditional supply chains (such as good strawberries or tree-ripened stone fruit) are reason enough for anyone seriously interested in food health and quality, cooking and flavour to want to work with their own garden.

If you've ever picked peas or broad beans from the plant and eaten them right there on the spot and noticed their juices, sugars and underlying slight creamy texture, and then tried the same thing later, after they have been harvested for a day or even a few hours, you would have noticed that those sugars change dramatically and the legumes become starchy and tough, even crumbly. This is simply a natural process that lots of produce goes through once the lifeline of the plant, roots and soil have been removed, and something that, as consumers of store-bought food, we have unfortunately just become accustomed to.

For the sake of food quality, and certainly from the perspective of cooking and consuming, I would say that this 'natural process' is a big negative. Sure, you can't grow everything, and using produce grown organically and close by is better than more industrial alternatives, but by working closely with our own vegetable garden we try to minimize the natural aging and breaking down of some foods before we have a chance to prepare, cook and serve them to our guests. As a result – or, at least, this is the intention – the fruit and veg are more vibrant, more textural and more flavoursome.

For us, working on the land helps us to feel more connected to the place, and nurturing the produce gives us a stronger connection to it as we prepare it for our guests. It also inspires respect for the area in which we live, and the work of the other local producers whose food we use at Brae. When we tend our produce, we are aware that the work we do in the kitchen begins here, in the garden, and the quality of both is important to resulting dishes we serve to our guests. And when we harvest, we are guided by the moment – what is ready to be harvested – more than anything else.

Making it work

One of the key factors with running an intensive kitchen garden is to be realistic about production. We run a fairly organized garden operation, with annual and seasonal plans in place outlining varieties to plant, seasonal notes and production needs and expectations. We operate in a manner that combines tradition, technology and science, employing techniques such as biological pest control, composting, green manure and crop rotation rather than synthetic fertilizers and pesticides, yet we still have crop failures, the normal water and available space issues and, of course, climatic and seasonal variations that play a part in determining what we actually achieve – not to mention a high cost of labour (or, more to the point, probably a lack of actual labour), being integral to any organic system.

There's lots of talk of restaurants with gardens growing everything they need, but the truth is it's very difficult to supply a busy restaurant twelve months of the year with all that's required. With climate change becoming more of an issue in

Australia, and with even the more predictable seasonal weather variations resulting in high and low production periods, it's important to be aware of your capabilities and to also understand your objectives and needs.

After quite bit of trial and error and, with hindsight, probably a good amount of of time and space wasted on unnecessary plantings and projects, I've decided to focus our priorities on certain things that have value for our cuisine and also for Brae as a business. Of course, there are the 'art projects' every season, with small trials to test and taste, but more and more, I've scaled down the baggage so we can consistently cope with the volumes of produce that the restaurant demands.

So at Brae now we tend to focus our current production efforts on a couple of key categories. They include uncommon ingredients that are not in the marketplace because there is little demand for them, but which have great gastronomic appeal and, therefore, are of interest to us as cooks and to our guests. We also grow ingredients that do not hold or travel well when ripe due to their delicate nature (so their texture or overall quality is compromised by transportation), and ingredients we feel we can't buy at a better quality from a trusted organic or biodynamic source locally. And we also produce ingredients that can be financially restrictive to have on the menu in the size and/or quantity that we require.

When deciding on how and what to spend our time on with the vegetable programme we're lucky that some of what we like and need can be found in our immediate location. We're surrounded by many specialist small farms in the Otways that are usually owned and run by people who have the skill, time and means to produce food better than we can and so, when it's appropriate, I'll choose to buy food from them. Apart from supporting the local economy and participating in providing a marketplace for food diversity, we find we're exposed to a community of people who are as interested and passionate about their ingredients as we are. Pick-your-own berry farms, farm-gate vegetable stalls and heritage apple orchards are all in our immediate vicinity, and olives, walnuts and potatoes are all grown commercially and sold within a ten-kilometre radius of the restaurant. Also, private growers, people with a small property and personal food-growing interests, often arrive at the kitchen door with a small bucket or car-boot load of something in absolutely pristine condition, picked just before making the call.

We've met several people that way who now supply us with ingredients – from tree-ripened limes (impossible to find in a Victorian market) to green almonds and super-fragrant quinces – and it's usually these guys who have the very best produce. Theirs is super-small production, and they are tending to their 'hobby' on a daily basis, and they wouldn't dare use chemicals as they are eating the same food themselves and have picked the produce with their own hands.

One interesting and important discovery that has come to me by having daily contact and interaction with our vegetable gardens is the ability to be much more courageous and spontaneous with dishes for the menu. Of course, many menu ideas start in my head at random times and, for these, there are the necessary testing and recipe development processes but, over the years, I've found that a large proportion of any menu we serve is made up of dishes that just happen and live more in the moment. Often, these dishes are ones that I feel I could never have imagined, but rather just occurred to me because I was in the right place at the right time and allowed the ingredients to do their thing. A chilled broth of broad beans and strawberries, fig leaf and yogurt whey only existed because those ingredients were growing relatively close to each other in last spring's garden, and so they all suddenly seemed completely logical together. Of course, we needed to infuse the whey and we made an oil infused with fig leaf too, but at the heart of it the inspiration came from being in the garden at that moment on that day, tasting one thing then another whilst smelling the aroma of another. The opportunity for this type of inspiration is a common and daily experience for those of us who work in this manner. Interestingly, too, I think there's a lot of merit in the idea of food that grows well together eating well together, and many classic cuisines have developed traditional recipes based on this concept. Tomatoes and basil?

We find we're exposed to a community of people who are as interested and passionate about their ingredients as we are.

Brae Gardens

One interesting and important discovery that has come to me by having daily contact and interaction with our vegetable gardens is the ability to be much more courageous and spontaneous with dishes for the menu.

Working closely with a garden also allows us, and even encourages us, to use parts of the plants that we could never find in a market or through a supplier. The tops of purple cauliflower, bolting in the late spring heat, would undoubtedly be removed from most commercial market gardens as a failed crop. But for us with our small, focused dishes, it's an opportunity to toast them in a little oil to serve with salt-baked green garlic and buttermilk left over from lightly churned cultured cream, not to mention the flowers and seed pods used in many spring and summer dishes that are often harvested well past the prime of a plant's life.

But it can't be all take. Intensive vegetable growing is environmentally taxing and, no matter how much you rotate crops, without sound planning and management it won't be long before you have more failures than successes. Without giving back to the earth much more than you take out, the land becomes tired and unproductive. For a kitchen that relies on the ability to be spontaneous by picking and choosing from abundance, if plant diversity isn't there it doesn't take long for creativity and inspiration to slow down, too.

As a means to stay on top of this, and particularly over time, as I've become more familiar with organic principles, we've changed the way in which we view the vegetable garden and the vegetables themselves. Of course we need them – the menus are full of them – but, more so, we need the land to be healthy so it can continue to provide for us.

I no longer view the vegetables we harvest as the most important part of the cycle and, for me, they are now more like a positive by-product rather than the main event of our production efforts. Our real interest is no longer focused on what we take out but more to do with what we put in, and rather than just growing vegetables we now see ourselves as more vested in growing soil – you could say we're simple dirt farmers!

From a cook's perspective and not that of a horticulturalist, it may be difficult to fully comprehend the impact soil health can have on flavour. Unless you've seen and tasted on a daily basis the difference that healthy organic soil can make to the flavour of food, it may even seem unbelievable, but let's use the example of a mushroom to illustrate the idea. Why do wild mushrooms have more flavour than cultivated ones? Is it simply that the varieties that grow wild are more flavoursome, or is it the soil or conditions in which they grow? I have no hesitation in saying that I believe a cultivated strain of mushroom grown in a wild environment such as a forest floor would develop more flavour.

A forest floor must be one of the best examples of a humus-rich, biologically diverse, continually active organic soil machine there is. All the time the topsoil is being fed by falling leaves and, as these break down and work their way into the subsoil, new material is being added to the surface. This is the same system we apply to our garden beds with the intention of not only improving the health and diversity of the soil but also the flavour of the vegetables grown in it, as with the mushroom example above.

To do this we're continually making compost, which, by definition, is soil. And to do this in the volumes we have to make a lot. But all that we need is mostly all here on site. We mow lawns every week and save the clippings, we keep all the green waste from the kitchen in two separate containers (one goes straight to compost, and one with softer greens to feed our hens). The soiled straw from the chicken bedding also goes in. We prune trees in our orchards, we pull weeds from the garden, and we collect leaves after sweeping paths, ash from the wood fire and chargrill, coffee grinds – the lot. Every now and then we add composted cow manure from a neighbour's property to give it a kick and, rather than drying all the grass we cut each spring for hay, we add a percentage of the fresh-cut paddock grass, too. All of this from our property or our neighbour's breaks down and goes back into the soil.

A typical day in the garden for the kitchen team
Each morning after the various group jobs are completed in the kitchen, the team breaks away into their sections and, under the direction of one of the senior chefs

de partie, around half the team goes out to complete the daily pick. They move as one, generally picking or harvesting a single product at a time so that quality and numbers can be monitored whilst picking at speed. Compostable items from the day before are added to the compost, eggs are collected, vegetable trimmings are fed to the chickens, along with some grain, their water is topped up and they are let out of their tractors to free range in a netted area amongst the fruit and olive trees. The kitchen team move quickly, putting softer, more delicate items straight into containers resting on ice in the warmer months so that they are not heat-affected, and picking early enough so that the heat of the day doesn't start to wilt the softer greens.

Root vegetables are first washed on site under taps in the garden, so that not too much soil is brought back into the kitchen, and unusable vegetable tops like larger carrots and older beets or broccoli leaves affected by white moth are trimmed there and then and placed straight into the compost.

As the work draws to an end, one or two chefs remain in the garden, finishing off anything to be picked in a small quantity that does not need the extra hands and muscle that a group provides, such as a few white strawberries for a special menu or a single artichoke to replace a dish for a guest with dietary restrictions.

After around one to one-and-a-half hours, depending on the day, weather and season and what volumes are required, any harvesting tools are returned to the shed and the chefs all return, get changed into kitchen whites and distribute the day's produce to the various sections for preparation and cooking.

That evening after service, clean down and the nightly briefing, the next day's menus are discussed and a new garden list is created. Any issues or concerns regarding the quality of certain ingredients, such as insect problems or shortfalls in required volumes, are brought to the attention of the sous chef and then I usually investigate and make necessary amendments to the menus in the morning.

With regard to seasonal plantings, general maintenance, weed and pest control, compost management, soil health and any irrigation issues, the two gardeners we currently employ handle the bulk of the work. We're fortunate that Brae has grown quite quickly in its first two years, and given the vegetable gardens are such a high priority, having skilled gardeners is obviously imperative to our success. We opened in December 2013 with just one gardener working only twelve hours a week and, prior to that, for the four months we had the property, myself, Jules and my father-in-law did all the initial maintenance and planting for the opening menus. I do love spending time in our gardens, but hopefully, the days of me weeding asparagus alone in spring rain for nine or ten hours at a stretch are a thing of the past.

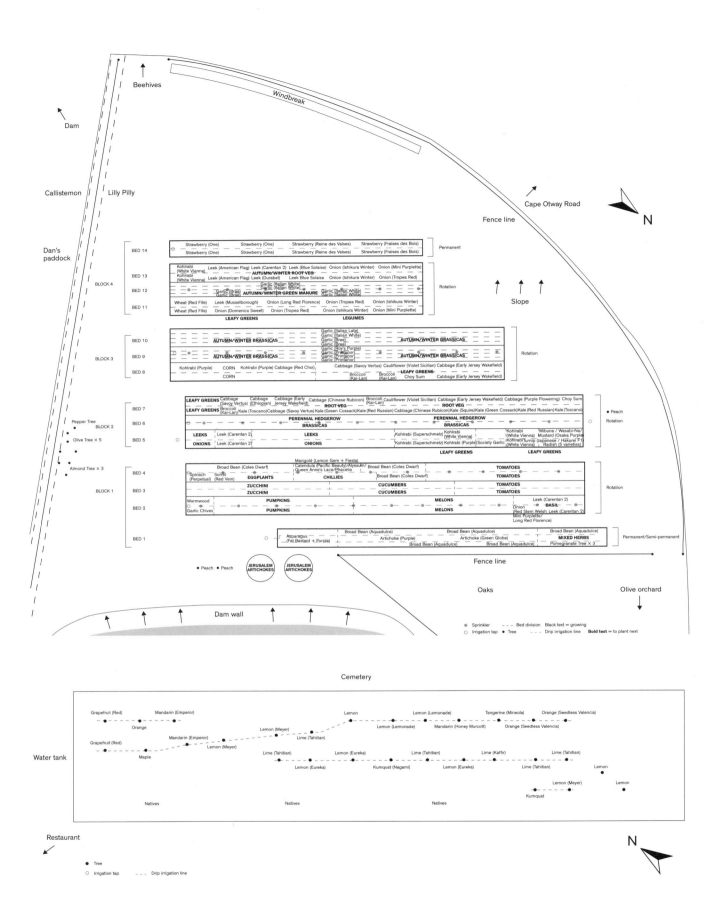

Top: Vegetable garden. Bottom: Citrus orchard

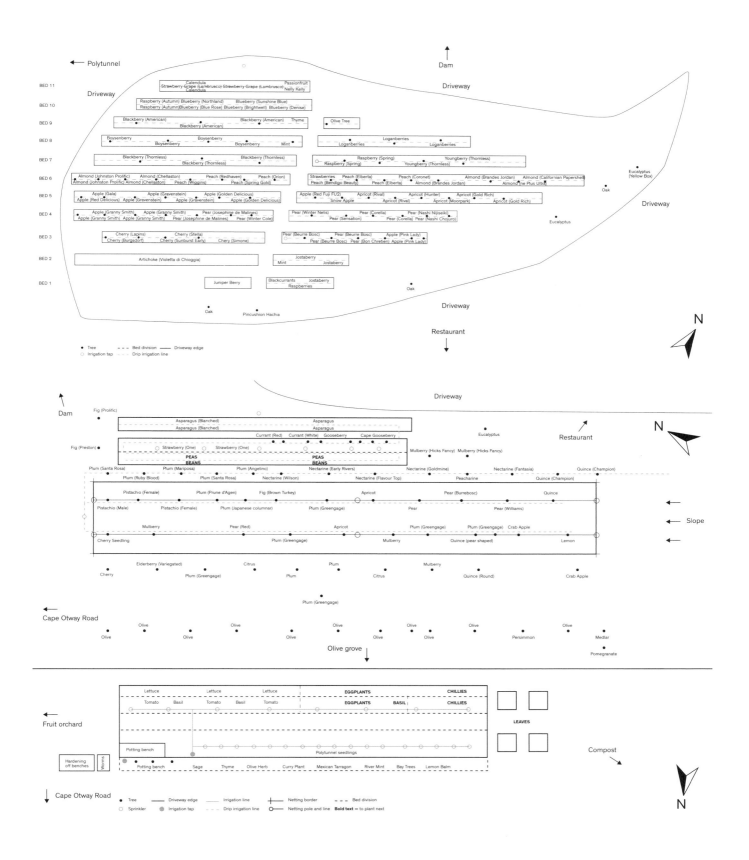

Top: New orchard. Bottom: Fruit trees, olives and polytunnel

Bread and Oven

Bread and Oven

Bread and Oven

Bread and Oven

I've always loved bread. Even as a kid, growing up on a typical Australian 'white bread' diet in the 1970s, I wouldn't pass through a single day without eating at least one slice, most likely toasted, before I left the house in the morning. These days, for me, though, the more flavoursome, darker coloured and less refined the bread, the better.

I've been baking bread at least five days a week for the best part of ten years now and it's never turned out the same twice. I note a slight nuance on the day before, with each individual loaf having its own identity, even when the recipe may not have changed for up to a year. I've never settled on a recipe that I think is the one. It's something that is always evolving: a little more water, a longer autolyse, less or more sieved flour, fresh milled or not; colder fermentation, hotter fermentation, longer fermentation, shorter fermentation. Seriously, I'm in awe of the many bakers around the world who pump out dozens of uniform, naturally fermented, hand-shaped loaves each day, as I consider natural bread-baking to be up there as one of the single most difficult things any cook can do consistently. Yet it is also one of the most rewarding jobs and the easiest to get excited about. I cannot imagine not baking bread and even think that, when I'm too old to move around a kitchen and be of any use in a service, I'll still bake bread.

Within our value system at Brae, the bread we serve, and the butter for that matter, have great significance. For me, bread is one of those societal measuring sticks: it's a cornerstone of many cuisines and has significant importance in the story of our civilisation. It's eaten in most households, in daily school lunches, has religious importance – obviously, the list goes on, as bread is one of those foods that has always been there for all people, regardless of their socioeconomic situation. Bread can be baked at home, from easily obtainable ingredients, yet the local baker has always been held in high regard and seen as integral to the social fabric of any town or suburb.

I'm interested in these types of foods that are ingrained in our cultures, as they are often the things people remember. A restaurant's cuisine can be totally authentic and creative, yet commonly, the moments that guests remember often involve something that they can relate to, are comfortable with and that have a place within their own value system. It's these things, the things you get served in nearly every restaurant or eat daily, that are often the most difficult to make an impact with, because they are nearly always subconsciously benchmarked against another version of that food eaten at some other time.

Along with having new and surprising food experiences at Brae, I want our guests to experience some of the best versions of things they already know – whether it be the longest-flavoured beef, deepest-flavoured chicken broth, most fragrant strawberry or sweetest garlic. These are comforts, and in a menu like ours which sets out to challenge and provoke along the way, I think it's the care taken with common or comfort foods that keeps the menu grounded. Hopefully, they help to provide the feeling of care and safety to our guests that is all tied up with the type of hospitality I want them to experience while being on this property and at the table in this farmhouse.

I'm very lucky that when we took over the property we inherited a masonry oven designed by the late Alan Scott. Alan was renowned the world over as a master oven builder and spent time on this property some fifteen years ago with the previous owners, running a weekend class for a small group who built the oven. The oven is heated by direct firing, meaning a fire is lit in the same chamber where the baking takes place and, during the course of extended firing, heat is stored deep within the masonry. The cleverness of the design results in a beautiful radiant heat once the fire is removed and the ash is cleaned out.

Inheriting this oven was one of the catalysts when it came to making decisions about the direction of cooking and food I wanted to serve at Brae – which I hope, by the way, is quite a natural, environmentally aware cuisine existing within the means of its surrounds. Building a fire every day, chopping wood from fallen timber from around the property, cleared (as any responsible landowner must do in Australia to reduce fire risk over the hotter months), and then the remaining ash cooled and kept to work into compost, which in turn is worked into the soil, while the preserved heat stored deep in the masonry is used to cook other menu items such as ducks, or to dry vegetables overnight for various seasonings – all this is bound together, as a type of closed-loop sustainable food system. The land's resources are being used effectively multiple times in multiple ways before becoming part of the land again, while providing for those on the land.

The land's resources are effectively being used multiple times in multiple ways before becoming part of the land again.

Bread recipe
This is the current process for the bread we serve at Brae.

Day 1
Feed the starter – 100 per cent freshly milled whole wheat flour (50 per cent sifted/50 per cent unsifted) mixed with rainwater at a ratio of 1:1 and left to ferment for 24 hours at around 18°C (64°F).
    Mill flour, sifting 40 per cent of the final weight (60 per cent whole wheat, 40 per cent sifted whole wheat) – let the freshly milled flour cool to less than 24°C (75°F) before combining at 85 per cent hydration with filtered rainwater. Leave to hydrate for 8 hours at around 18°C (64°F).

Day 2
Combine starter and hydrated flour and let stand for 1 hour before adding salt and combining by hand into a dough. Leave in a sealed plastic container, keeping the internal temperature of the dough between 21 and 23°C (70 and 73°F) and never letting it rise above 24°C (75°F). Fold the dough over itself every half an hour for 2 hours, and then on the hour for 2 hours. At the end of the second hourly fold, transfer the dough onto a bench then cut and pre-shape into 1kg pieces. Let stand for between half an hour and an hour, then complete the final folds and shaping before placing in floured proofing baskets. Place these into the refrigerator at between 2 and 4°C (36 and 39°F) and leave for 20-22 hours.

Day 3
Fire the oven, starting at the front with a small fire and then, as it catches, add more timber, burning it all the way to the back before spreading it out all over the hearth – this takes around 2½ hours in an oven that is fired every day. Sweep and mop the oven clean then close the door to let the heat become evenly distributed throughout the chamber: the oven at this stage must be at around 340°C (644°F) on the hearth from front to back, with the air temp a little hotter. The prolonged baking temperature needs to sit at around 250°C (482°F), which the oven will drop to when the 11 × 1kg loaves are added. Remove the bread from the refrigerator, then score the loaves and load them in before spraying about 100ml water into the chamber and the door. Wet a towel, wring it out so that it's damp but not wet, then use it to cover the inside of the door before closing it again (letting it steam into the oven while it dries from the heat). Once dry (around 7 minutes), remove the towel from the door, and give the chamber another quick spray of water, then close the door and leave the bread to bake for around 45 more minutes (around 1 hour in total). Check after around 20 minutes for any hot spots on the hearth that may burn the bottoms of the loaves and move them around if necessary. Once baked, dark and delicious, remove the loaves and leave them to cool on racks to room (or outside) temperature before serving.

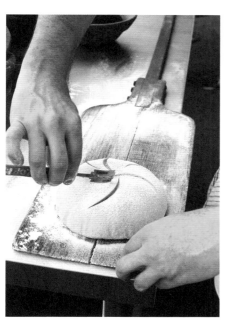

<u>Diary</u>

Diary

December 11th – Thursday

First day back after Tuesday's first-year birthday party and staff Christmas party – a strangely quieter week coming up, after having six to eight weeks in a row of each week being our busiest week. Will take a bit to keep the team motivated for the tail end of the year before the well-earned Christmas holiday break. A sunny day, but a surprisingly quiet night – only sixteen booked. A new dish tonight, using the first of our new potatoes and flathead roe with cured egg, milk and mustard. Just-harvested potatoes that taste of the soil and don't see the refrigerator – another great example of simple luxury and why we have a garden. Drove to St Leonards (1½ hours) just before service and after the bread was baked to pick up a long-overdue piece of equipment for the property, a fire fighting tank/trailer – 1,000 litres with a four-stroke water pump and 30 metres fire hose. This is hopefully something that will never be used, but when you're surrounded by grass and have a large compost on site, it's imperative to have something for emergencies. As a bonus, this tank and pump will come in handy for watering all the new native trees and proposed landscaped areas of the property that don't have water running to them. Straightforward service, but the lemon and blackberry dessert tastes all out of whack for some reason – all the acid's gone and it's too sweet.

December 12th – Friday

Busy lunch but quiet dinner – after several weeks of being full all the time you can tell it's getting that bit closer to Christmas and people are spending time with family or friends. Lunch was two groups of work Christmas parties and a few other tables. Warm day with a bit of wind, which always makes the barbecue a bit of fun. Had the ducks on for lunch – aged for ten days – I think I prefer them a little drier, at around fourteen days dry-aged and maybe even in winter and spring, when they have them on pears as well as pasture, rather than their current diet of strawberries. Bread playing up again due to increase in heat too – would be good to have a bread proofer at some stage instead of always having to look around for the spot with the right temperature. Good to see Shane back this week after being walkabout for a couple, as he can get on with some serious weeding and a few odd spots on the property that have been ignored for a while – like mowing the driveway on lot one and a general tidy up of the spots I haven't had time to get to in the last couple of weeks. I much prefer it when I don't have to be head lawn-mower! The new potatoes and milk skin dish is not quite there either – looking forward to getting some sea urchins next week to sort it out, although the cream we made by cooking white onions in whey and then adding flathead roe before blitzing with cider vinegar is delicious. Lemon and blackberry dessert is back on track but interesting to note how the citrus is losing acidity as the temperature warms ups – just shows how much you have to keep your eye on things as they change throughout the season – whoever said there are only four seasons obviously hasn't spent much time cooking out of a garden.

December 13th – Saturday

Hot day – in the thirties. Transplanted some of the plants in the landscaped area out the front of the restaurant yesterday and probably shouldn't have due to the heat – hope they make it. Almost full at lunch and every table booked at dinner. Had ducks again at lunch with quandongs and dried liver. The nasturtium flowers we soak in mead vinegar (from honey grown at Brae) and then chargrill to add a really great touch to this dish. At dinner, a relatively smooth and quick service, although many tables left the dining room to walk outside at dusk and admire the killer sunset. One of the great things about summer at Brae is dining in the evening, arriving in daylight and being able to watch the amazing sunsets we get nearly every night – the west view out of the main dining room and kitchen windows is pretty special.

Full-blood Tajima beef raised 100 per cent on pasture and then aged for forty days was the last savoury at dinner service, with dried cauliflower, onions cooked in whey and grilled leaves and flowers. I would serve beef more often if it could taste like this – a depth from the grass and dry-aging and then slowly barbecued over red gum – was really well received.

Lots of jostaberries and blackcurrants now ripe in the garden, which are being used on the red fruits and lemon dessert – the currants have this incredible her-baceous note that reminds me of juniper, and I'm thinking to myself, is it because they are growing near each other? We're lightly poaching them in a sugar syrup infused with lemon, lime and grapefruit.

Shane got a good amount done too – getting some compost around the orna-mental trees and giving them a good water. We've also planted a lot of natives lately to screen the new veggie garden and the block of land that the accommo-dation is going on, as well as the other block where we'll build a house. Shane got the last of the guard/protectors around the new trees and gave them a good water – they're only young and a day like today with a warm wind and temps in the thirties dries them out pretty quick.

Did have to turn the sprinklers on all the veg garden beds tonight too – first time for a couple of weeks.

December 14th – Sunday
Not a Brae thing but our daughter Ivy was up with a fever all night – not much sleep for Jules and not heaps for me, either. Got in, baked the bread, checked menus with Damien and then went to Colac to get some medicine for Ivy. Restaurant was well under way with lunch by the time I got back. Ducks coming out and getting smoked and most things under control. Staff motivation is unfortu-nately well down and I can really feel myself becoming more and more frustrated at the moment with silly little mistakes – I had a feeling having the staff Christmas party two weeks out from the end of the year may have this type of effect, where everyone, or so it seems, has decided that all the details are too hard and they've clocked off for the year.

A few local tables in for lunch, along with a couple who had been to Royal Mail when I was there, so lots of chit-chat with the generally happy punters after service.

Fed the chooks and watered them, turned the sprinklers on for twenty minutes or so and then popped home to check on Ivy, who finally had some of the medicine at around 4.30 p.m. and so had chirped up a bit.

Dinner – a couple of industry tables, a couple of gourmands and a few precious ones – typical service, really. Must say that, along with all of the staff I too am looking forward to the ten-day break over Christmas and New Year.

December 15th – Monday
Muggy and overcast with a bit of late rain today. Was good to get some plants into the native garden beds – Kangaroo Paws and Grevilleas. Mulched a few of the ornamental trees and then had to go to Colac to get the ride-on mower wheel fixed. Jostaberries are certainly in full swing, as are potatoes. Asparagus still pushing on, and lots of dill, olive plant, fennel tops, chive and onion flowers and tarragon. Saw the first of the courgette (zucchini) flowers starting to appear and will definitely have to find a use for them over the next few weeks.

December 18th – Thursday
First day of the last week before the Christmas break and for 2014! Full dinner service with journos, bloggers and general VIPs everywhere. We served the first of the season's Southern Rock Lobster, or crayfish as they're known in Victoria, with the new potato and flathead roe dish, which worked well – poach the tails,

> I love the way that you discover things that work so well and seem so obvious, yet you may never have the chance to imagine them – purely right-place-at-right-time cuisine.

boil the heads and pick all the meat, then barbecue the meat over red gum charcoal – really delicious. Crays are one of the real quality crustaceans out of the Southern Ocean and particularly off the Great Ocean Road out of towns from Apollo Bay all the way through to Portland and beyond. We like them at around 1.5 kg and the gaminess they develop as they get a bit bigger is pretty delicious too – I'm a real sucker for barbecued crays.

Picked up around thirty new native plants this morning before the rain – some more Muntries and a type of native mint I hadn't seen before that's super-fragrant – it will be a nice addition along the path to the front door – hopefully the aromatics will help guests to relax. I think they smell delicious and quite soothing. The gardens out the front are finally filling out, I can't wait for a couple of years from now as it starts to lush out.

Paul did quite a bit of planting this week and also ran some water to the plantation area that will screen the new accommodation from our block – this will eventually act as a nature corridor, giving birds and bees a place to hang out and eat from on their way to the veggie garden.

Over the weekend I tried some of the bobby veal that a local dairy producer who also grows shiitakes is trying out. I enjoyed it and can definitely see a place for it on the menu in the future – it certainly would be appropriate at this time of year. We ate it with about fifteen of the first zucchini flowers that will unfortunately hit full bloom just as we go on our Christmas break at the end of the week – it's always the way.

Did the chilled broth of broad bean, green almond and strawberry, fig leaf and yogurt whey tonight, also for a VIP table. Such a killer flavour combination for this time of year and so unusual but completely instinctive when you're eating it – certainly something that's come out of spring and early summer this year that I'm proud of. It was quite spontaneous too. I love the way that, by planting produce and then spending time in the garden eating different things that ripen together, you discover things that work so well and seem so obvious, yet you may never have the chance to imagine them – purely right-place-at-right-time cuisine.

December 19th – Friday
A pretty stock standard (busy) day.

December 30th–Jan 5th
I came back from a few days break early so I could assess the property before the others started and the wedding booked in for Jan 2nd. What a mess – we've had serious winds over the last couple of days and some hot days. The lack of rain this spring is really starting to show, with all the dams low and paddocks browned off. There's fallen trees and shit lying around everywhere and I instantly get the feeling that it's better never to leave for more than a day or two, otherwise things get away. I'm actually a bit depressed at the sight of the property and although we worked so hard last year trying to plant, regenerating certain areas with native plants and creating nature corridors for native birds and wildlife, the place still seems so far from being anywhere near where we want it to be and I know we've got years ahead of us before we start to really see the property how I imagine it to be.

I got in early on the 31st and started mowing so it's done. Shane will come in on the 1st and morning of the 2nd to do the final touches of the tidy up. There's lots of weeds in the veggie garden beds and I also planted around twenty-five new native plants in the gardens by the front door and restaurant windows, which is always a work in progress. I really didn't like the plant selection we went with at the time of the renovation and have spent the last six months improving it with flowering species that are also nice to look at.

Damien is around doing bits and pieces to get ready and he seems keen just to get back to work. On New Year's Eve I did a few hours around the place, went for a surf at around dusk and then just went home, ate some Dorper lamb grown on the property with the first zucchini flowers from the garden (of which there are

Diary

millions) and had an early night, knowing that in the morning I'd need to come in and get the bread organized ready to bake the next day as we're heading for total fire bans over the weekend, with temps expected to be over 40 degrees and a strong northerly blowing.

The wedding on the 2nd went smoothly, although it was 35 degrees. We adjusted the menu so we could get ahead for the first official day back on the 3rd. The bookings for Jan are really crazy and we'll end up doing close to 1,100 covers with lots of services full. We're using bread that we froze before Christmas, flashing it through the brick oven after the bake. This way we have bread for Saturday, which has already been declared a total fire ban day. I checked the fire equipment before going home on Friday – starting the generator and testing the fire hose and pressure.

The 3rd was a nightmare – full lunch and full dinner – total fire ban so we had to bring my Kamado barbecue from home and roast the pork and all the charred vegetable garnishes in the kitchen – it's actually lucky I have it. It does seem quite dangerous outside, with winds hitting the 100 kilometres an hour mark before a crazy late change from the south that resulted in lightning and heaps of trees and branches crashing around the property. We did consider lighting the fire in the morning to bake bread but at 6.30 a.m., with hot crazy winds, I decided it was too dangerous and instead we put fire bricks in the oven and heated them over a few hours, trying to create a situation similar to the hearth in the brick oven – unfortunately, it's not quite the same.

Sunday a cool change came through, thankfully, and we're back to both baking in the wood oven and grilling outside – just how we like it.

January 8th – Thursday
Blessed with some cool weather and actual ground-wetting rain today, with more to come over the next few days – you can water all you like, but nothing wets gardens like rain. All the fruit trees sighed with relief. Unfortunately, the rain was a bit late for most of the berries. They all just dropped off last week in the heat – masses on the bushes one day and then literally nothing the next and, unfortunately, with the dams so low at this time of year, we just can't keep watering. Three stagiaires this week, which is great. It's busy so they'll get to see loads, and having them here always improves staff morale in the kitchen. We're going to construct the new red gum sleeper beds in the courtyard early next week, so Shane will be knocking out the really shit old brickwork that's been pissing us off since we first saw the property – it is good to see some progress and finally get to the things that really look shit.

January 9th – Friday
Fourteen tables and full for lunch, fourteen tables and full for dinner – big one!!

January 15th – Thursday
Was the busiest week we've ever had last week, with some hot days, but every service handled pretty well. It does put a strain on the garden, and this week it feels like we are again behind on production. Was an amazing day on Tuesday, though, and although I was supposed to be putting in the new sleeper walls in the courtyard with Paul it was nice to be at home watching all that rain falling. Was probably the most rain in a day for over a year and with 45 milimetres in twenty-four hours it really made a difference. All drinking water tanks were overflowing and lots of water running into the dams and, of course, saturating the garden beds and paddocks – amazing!!

Following that, we spent the next day and a half constructing the new garden beds out the back of the restaurant – putting in red gum sleeper walls. They're looking good and I can't wait to start planting in them. It's certainly one area of the property that has been neglected to date, simply because we can't do everything at once. Good service tonight – quick and without cock-ups!

Blessed with some cool weather and actual ground-wetting rain today... All the fruit trees sighed with relief.

January 16th – Friday

Some strange weather again – lots of wind for this time of year, so all the rain from earlier in the week has basically dried up. Ducks back on today and they're not the best we've seen – aged ten days but in a weird spot between too fatty and not dry enough, with a flavour that hasn't developed the right length yet. Hopefully they'll improve over the next few days.

Used lots of zucchini and squash flowers for the snacks, stuffing the prawn and tamarind mix inside them. Mussels came in – sea bounty down at Portarlington – nice and plump and really good flavour, although the couple I tasted today were a bit tough. Working on a dish of charred beet broth with mussels that we've been throwing about. Was fortunate to go out on one of the boats a couple of years ago with Ben Shewry and a few others and realized after some instruction from the guys on the boat that the typical commercial kitchen method of opening mussels by dumping them into a pot that's almost buckling it's so hot is completely detrimental to the quality of the mussels, and just bringing them to a gentle simmer slowly, completely submerged in water, is far more appropriate to maintaining their plump texture and water content. We've opened them that way ever since, pulling them out of the slowly heating liquid one by one as they open and removing the beards then, when they release them without a struggle.

January–February

In the end, Jan this year was a massive month, with not a lot of menu changes as we struggled to keep up with the numbers – full lunch into full dinner all the way up till Australia Day on the 26th.

Around the property we've struggled a little, with the lack of rain in spring last year taking its toll on our water reserves. All dams are right down, and in the second week of Feb we actually had to remove the line from the windmill and start pumping water up to the central dam – this is obviously quicker than the windmill but we go through around three litres of fuel every three hours so I'm not sure if it's worth it.

We've made significant inroads with the sleeper walls around the house too, nearly all the way round. Added composted cow manure from Reynors and started planting. There's probably one or two days left to finish construction now, but we've run out of sleepers for the moment. Plenty of continued native plant planting also, and the indigenous edible garden is certainly growing by the week – Muntries, ruby saltbush, river mint, lemon myrtle, native pepper (Otways), lilly pilly, Warrigal greens, bunya bunya, are all growing well.

Planning application has also been approved for the accommodation and we'll get stuck into that this year – six rooms that fit in with us nicely.

February 12th – Thursday

Finally met up with Don Lidgerwood today to discuss the possibility of a grain crop (probably spelt and maybe red wheat) on lot one of the property, and also on the newly subdivided block. He's had a bit of success in recent years growing various heirloom wheat crops on his property two kilometres away, and he and George Biron actually had a pretty good result from a crop several years ago before we bought the place. It's been on the agenda since we took over, so it's great to get the ball rolling. As the bread has been a real focus in the kitchen, and with our intention of expanding production to have a retail food store, I've been really keen to grow the grain we use on site and possibly sell a good organically grown heirloom wheat to any artisanal bakers out there in Melbourne, or closer, who may be interested. Apparently Don has a stone mill he hasn't fired up yet and although he's milling quite finely at the moment he did seem keen on my intention of milling whole wheat for our bread. If all goes to plan we should sow the first crop within a couple of months and grow it slowly over winter for a spring/summer harvest.

It was nice to see the garden standing tall today and a flick of green through the paddocks.

February 13th and 14th – Friday and Saturday

Hot morning with a massive dry storm blowing in lightning strikes around lunch time to a half-full restaurant, causing the power to go out for two and a half hours. No aircon, no extraction fans, no music, no water (as we're on water pumps) – so no toilets flushing. Luckily we have rain water stored in large 25-litre jugs for drinking in the dining room and lucky we're cooking most things outside on the barbecue or in the masonry oven. No one really seemed to mind, thankfully, but it was a real bastard! Following that, though, we did get 45 milimetres of rain over the next 15 hours or so, which is incredible for this time of year. Unfortunately it won't do much to the dam's level, but it was nice to see the garden standing tall today and a flick of green through the paddocks. There has been significant veggie planting over the last week and a bit, so the rain will be put to good use.

February 17th, 18th and 19th – Tuesday, Wednesday and Thursday

Works continue! It's sort of relentless at the moment and I do wonder sometimes how it must be to just rent a building in the city and have a restaurant?

Had several tradies here the last three days over our weekend (bobcat operators and landscapers, in fact), dealing with the shitty driveway we inherited and putting in walking paths for people to get around the property – oh, and what I call the 'weed eradication programme' of removing some more of the plants/shrubs and small trees that provide absolutely nothing aesthetically to the property and have no positive effect on the landscape or nature (six truckloads this time). It's nice however to see the place slowly taking shape and opening out some longer views towards different parts of the property and surrounding hills. I reckon five years from now I'll be starting to feel like we are getting somewhere! Unfortunately, as with all land improvement works, nothing goes 100 per cent to plan and each time you remove something or work on an area there's the feeling that, rather than improve a space, you've just left a gaping hole that you need to mend. I know we've made massive improvements in creating a much more relevant landscape but it's not easy always to see it, especially when there are trucks and bobcats tearing up and down the drive 15 minutes before customers are supposed to arrive and about half a day after they're supposed to be finished.

Recipes

Recipes

A welcome: some snacks and bites

When you begin reading the menu at Brae we want to grab your attention, to let you know that you're going to be treated to a party, an occasion that hopefully flows with enough energy that it creates a rhythm. Our intention is to engage you from the get-go, to put you at ease so you feel like you're being looked after, but also, to get you excited about what's coming – even if you're not prepared for it. We want to take control and curate the next few hours of your life and hope that you'll want to come along for the ride.

As I've said before, this part of the menu – a little hit of seven to ten mini-dishes, mostly served without cutlery – which appears before we serve any bread and butter, is our way of the kitchen saying, 'Welcome to Brae, we've spent all morning getting all of this ready for you and we want you to enjoy yourselves – we're going to do all that we can to make your experience with us special'.

I hope this section of the menu feels like an opening act of sorts, before we settle into the nitty-gritty. You get to meet a few of the main characters of the season here, but some of the more complex storylines lie ahead.

Asparagus

For any dishes with asparagus at Brae, we use a technique of removing the outer fibre of the asparagus before cooking it, and it's always done with a sharp knife rather than a peeler, first removing the leaves and then starting on one side and working around the spear, peeling from the tip to the base in a straight, nonstop motion (rather than scratching). Instead of appearing manhandled and over-peeled, with lighter green or yellow marks on the skin where a peeler has been pressed too hard into the vegetable, the result is a beautiful even-coloured deep green with a fantastic clean, stringless texture. I've heard many cooks over time questioning why you would peel asparagus and, when you see it done badly, I tend to agree. But by using a knife, taking care and always starting at the very top of the spear just under the tip, and always peeling just the very outer fibre, the value of the result – the improved and refined texture of the asparagus, as well as its flavour after brief cooking – is, for me, unquestionable.

Asparagus, olive plant and sea butter

For 4 people

Sea lettuce powder
100g fresh sea lettuce
salt

Sea butter
4g sea lettuce powder (see above)
100g unsalted butter

Asparagus
4 spears of fat asparagus
salt

Olive plant (holly flax)
3–4 small olive plant leaves
    per piece of asparagus

For the sea lettuce powder
Wash the harvested sea lettuce in salted water, picking through it carefully to ensure all sand, shells and other debris are completely removed. It is important to wash the sea lettuce many times, and to give it a good soak in abundant water, as it holds a lot of grit.

Once the sea lettuce is completely free of any impurities, it is a good idea to taste it to check for salt content. If it is too salty, give it a quick soak in fresh water until the desired salt level is achieved.

To dry the sea lettuce, place it in a dehydrator and dry it at 55°C (131°F) for 6–12 hours. Process the dried sea lettuce in a food processor to a fine powder. It will hydrate readily, so this powder must be stored in an airtight container.

For the sea butter
Combine 4g of the sea lettuce powder with the butter, ensuring there are no lumps and that the mixture is homogenously blended. Reserve the butter, covered and refrigerated, until needed. Reserve the remaining sea lettuce powder in an airtight container for other preparations.

For the asparagus
With a sharp turning knife and starting at the tip of the asparagus, peel the first fibre off each piece. It is important to peel in one motion from top to bottom, ensuring you do not peel too deeply or scratch the stems, leaving the chlorophyll intact.

For the olive plant
Remove the olive plant leaves from the plant. Wash them in chilled water and pat dry on absorbent paper. Store in an airtight container until needed.

To serve
Warm the sea butter in a saucepan, allowing it to melt but not brown.

Blanch the asparagus in boiling water with a ratio of 10g salt per litre of water. The asparagus should be just cooked with a little crunch.

Add the asparagus spears to the butter and gently coat them. Remove the spears and transfer to a serving plate. Cover each spear with olive leaves.

83

Asparagus and prawn

For 4 people

Chlorophyll
300g baby spinach leaves

Crustacean powder
400g roasted and dehydrated
   prawn heads
2.5g sea lettuce powder
   (see page 82)

Asparagus
4 large asparagus spears
salt
olive oil

Charred asparagus purée
10 spears of large, fat asparagus
olive oil
0.5g gellan gum
chlorophyll from spinach
   (see above)

To finish
8 three-cornered leek flowers

For the chlorophyll
Wash the spinach and process it in
a juicer. Place the strained spinach juice
in a saucepan and stir over medium heat
until it reaches 70°C (158°F). At this
temperature the solid chlorophyll will
separate from the water. Working quickly
to avoid oxidisation, pass the juice through
a fine sieve (strainer). Discard the brown
liquid and keep the solid chlorophyll left in
the strainer. If the chlorophyll is too wet it
can be scraped over absorbent paper
several times with a spatula until sufficiently
dry. Store the resulting chlorophyll paste,
refrigerated, in an airtight container for
a maximum of 3 days.

For the crustacean powder
Combine the ingredients in a food
processor and process to a powder. Pass
the resulting powder through a fine sieve
(strainer), sifting out any large pieces.
Reserve in an airtight container.

For the asparagus
With a sharp turning knife and starting just
below the head of the asparagus, peel the
first fibre off each piece. It is important to
peel in one motion from top to bottom,
ensuring you do not peel too deeply or
scratch the stems.
   Blanch the asparagus in boiling water
with a ratio of 10g salt per litre of water.
Refresh the cooked spears in heavily iced
water. The asparagus should be just
cooked with some bite, but no crunch.

For the charred asparagus purée
Prepare a barbecue.
   Dress the asparagus spears lightly with
olive oil and chargrill them on the barbecue
until cooked and coloured evenly. Whilst
they are still hot, juice the asparagus.
For better yield, it's important to process
the pulp several times through the juicer
before discarding.
   Chill the juice rapidly and combine
it with gellan gum at a ratio of 0.5g to
every litre of juice.
   Transfer the juice to a Thermomix and,
using speed 5 setting, gently warm it to
95°C (203°F). Maintain this temperature
for 5 minutes.
   Transfer the juice to a chilled tray and
refrigerate it for approximately 3 hours until
the mixture has set and stabilised. Then
transfer the mixture to the Thermomix, add
the chlorophyll, using about 3g chlorophyll
for every 100g purée, and process quickly
on high speed. Season the mixture, then
transfer to a sealed container and keep
ready for service.

To finish
Gently warm the asparagus spears in
olive oil and season liberally with the
crustacean powder. Place a large spoonful
of the charred asparagus purée in the
centre of a each plate (to be used as
a dipping sauce) and arrange the spears
next to it. Scatter over the three-cornered
leek flowers.

Chicken and truffle sandwich

For 4 people

Fenugreek oil
140g fenugreek seeds
500ml olive oil

Chicken terrine
1kg chicken wings
fenugreek oil (see above), to cover
1g gold leaf gelatine
75ml reduced chicken stock,
  warmed

Fenugreek mayonnaise
4 egg yolks
5g Dijon mustard
10–20ml white wine vinegar
450ml fenugreek oil (see above)
20g chopped chives
salt, to taste
lemon juice, to taste

Truffle
1 large Australian winter truffle

For the fenugreek oil
Combine the seeds and oil in a vacuum
pack and heat at 70°C (158°F) for 3 hours.
Leave to cool naturally and leave at room
temperature for a minimum of 3 weeks
prior to using.

For the chicken terrine
Preheat the oven to 100°C (212°F).
  Joint the wings and place them in a
baking tray. Cover with fenugreek oil and
confit in the preheated oven for 3 hours
or until soft. Remove the wings from the
oil and, while still warm, pick off all the
meat. Pack 750g of the chicken meat into
a lined terrine mould or similar.
  Dissolve the gelatine in the hot chicken
stock and pour it over the chicken,
ensuring it works its way into any gaps.
Wrap the terrine with clingfilm (plastic
wrap), weight it heavily and refrigerate
overnight or until firm.

For the fenugreek mayonnaise
Combine the egg yolks, mustard and
vinegar and slowly whisk in the oil.
Season with salt and lemon juice then
fold in the chives.

For the truffle
Brush the truffle to remove any dirt
or impurities, then shave it into nice
large slices.

To serve
Carefully unmould the chicken terrine and
cut into rectangular pieces. Place a dollop
of mayonnaise on each piece of terrine,
then build 'sandwiches' using the truffle
slices as if they were bread, so you have
mayonnaise-topped chicken between 2
slices of truffle. Season with salt and serve.

Chicken broth and truffle toast

For 4 people

Croissant dough
Poolish preferment:
100ml water at 23°C (73°F)
0.1g instant yeast
100g plain (all-purpose) flour
Dough:
200ml water
500g plain (all-purpose) flour
75g caster sugar
15g salt
10g poolish (see above)
100g chilled butter, diced
To laminate:
330g chilled butter

Roast chicken broth
5kg chicken frames
400g white onions
250g carrots
3.5kg chicken wings
olive oil

Red Kuri pumpkin cream
100g Red Kuri pumpkin, diced
7.5g grapeseed oil
20ml water
40ml milk
7.5g barrel-aged mirin
salt
gellan gum

Barbecued brassicas
400g mixture of large brassica
  leaves, such as red kale, red
  choi, black cabbage, turnip tops,
  Chinese broccoli or Chinese
  cabbage
olive oil
salt

Almond praline
300g blanched and peeled
  almonds
200g caster sugar
65ml water →

For the croissant dough
To make the poolish, combine the water with the yeast in a bowl, then add the flour. Cover and leave to stand at room temperature for 8–12 hours or overnight.

To make the dough, first pour the water in around the poolish so that it can be removed from the bowl. Put the dry ingredients into the bowl of a stand mixer and add 10g of the poolish. Combine the ingredients on the lowest speed setting. Add the butter and continue to mix on the lowest speed setting for 2 minutes. Once combined, mix for a further 20 minutes. Remove the bowl from the mixer, cover the dough with a cloth and leave to prove for 20 minutes.

Roll out the butter for laminating between 2 sheets of greaseproof (wax) paper into a rectangle measuring 15cm × 20cm, with a thickness of 1cm. Keep the butter chilled in a refrigerator until you are ready to use it.

After the proving time has elapsed, roll out the dough into a rectangle a little larger than the butter. The longer edges should be parallel to the edge of your work surface. Place the butter on top of the dough so that it is centred, then roll the edges of the dough over the butter to bring them together in the centre of the rectangle and pinch them together to encase the butter. (The long sides of the rectangle are now perpendicular to the edge of the work surface.) Roll out the dough away from yourself, extending the longer sides, then turn the dough so that the longer sides are parallel to the edge of your work surface.

Imagine the dough divided into 3 equal sections. Fold the section to the right over the central section. Now fold the section at the left over the folded dough, making a book-like shape – this is 1 fold. Cover the dough to avoid it drying out and leave to rest for 30 minutes. Repeat the rolling and folding process a further 4 times, each time resting the dough between folds. Keep the dough and butter at a cool temperature.

After 5 rolls and rests, roll out the dough to a 50cm × 20cm rectangular sheet with a thickness of 5mm. Keep refrigerated until ready to use.

For the roast chicken broth
Make the roast chicken broth following the instructions on page 220.

For the Red Kuri pumpkin cream
Chop the pumpkin into small dice. Sweat it in the oil over a low heat until soft. Add the water, cover the pumpkin with a cartouche and steam until all the water has evaporated. Add the milk and bring it to the boil. Purée the pumpkin and milk in a food processor, then add the mirin and check the seasoning. Chill the mixture, then thicken it with gellan gum, using 0.6g gellan gum for every 100g purée. Transfer to a piping (pastry) bag and reserve in the refrigerator.

For the barbecued brassicas
Prepare a barbecue.

Dress the leaves with a little olive oil and then grill them over the barbecue, ensuring the heat level is high, allowing the leaves to brown a little. Season with salt and remove from the heat. Chop the leaves, removing any thick stems, then mix them together and check the seasoning.

For the almond praline
Preheat the oven to 140°C (285°F).

Put the almonds onto a baking tray and dry-roast for 20 minutes.

Combine the sugar and water in a wide-based saucepan and cook until the temperature reaches 116°C (240°F). Remove from the heat, immediately add the warm almonds and stir gently until the sugar crystallizes around the almonds.

Return the saucepan to the heat and, stirring continuously, gently caramelize the sugar to a deep, dark golden caramel, ensuring all the almonds are evenly coated. Immediately pour out the almond praline onto a Silpat and allow to cool.

Transfer the praline to a blast chiller and freeze to −30°C (−22°F). When completely frozen, process the praline to a fine powder. Store frozen until needed. →

Truffle toast
croissant dough (see page 88)
150g Comté cheese, grated
300g barbecued brassicas (see
    page 88), leaves, finely chopped
50g black truffle, finely chopped
30g almond praline (see page 88)
    grated zest of 1 large tree-
    ripened lemon
egg wash, for brushing
Red Kuri pumpkin cream (see
    page 88),
finely sliced truffle (allow 6–8
    slices per toast)
Note – this yields more truffle
toast than is required

To finish
lemon thyme leaves
5g chopped truffle per serve

For the truffle toast

One by one, cover the dough with the filling ingredients, starting with cheese, barbecued brassicas, chopped truffle and almond praline, then Microplane the lemon zest over the top. Roll up the dough into a log, ensuring sure that the filling inside it is firmly pressed and encased. Freeze the dough, then cut it into even 1.5-cm wide rounds. Lay out the slices on a Silpat and brush them with egg wash. Leave to prove at room temperature for 90 minutes.

Preheat the oven to 175°C (350°F).

Once the proving time has elapsed, brush the rounds again with egg wash, then bake for 25 minutes. Transfer the 'toasts' to a wire rack and leave to cool.

Spread pumpkin cream across the flat side (the side that was against the tray while baking) of each toast, then top with truffle rounds, arranging them so that they overlap slightly.

To finish

Warm the truffle toasts slightly under a salamander until the truffle warms and is aromatic. Heat the chicken broth.

Reserving a little of each ingredient, put lemon thyme leaves and chopped truffle into a small teapot and top up with hot chicken broth. Put a little of the reserved truffle and thyme in the cups that the broth will be served in.

Place the toasts onto plates and then pour the broth over the chopped truffle and thyme leaves in the cups while serving.

Burnt pretzel, treacle and pork, and salt and vinegar crisps

Don't get me wrong – there's nothing wrong with Champagne, and the tradition of drinking it to kick off any celebration, no matter how small or spontaneous, should be encouraged, particularly at the start of a meal after a long drive with potentially some pretty average food along the way (which is occasionally the case for some of our customers who have driven a good distance to be with us). Champagne is certainly still the preferred aperitif for most who arrive at the restaurant. But, at around the time Brae opened to the public, I was looking at the proposed menu and the types of ingredients we were serving (mostly everyday ingredients that we all have access to and can relate to) and thinking about the context in which we would be serving this menu (in a farmhouse, in rural Australia) and of my hope that our guests would feel welcomed and at home as if they'd been invited over, and I couldn't help thinking of the more common Australian social norm of 'having a beer'. It's the same thing I like to do at a lunch amongst friends or when invited to someone's house on a warm day. We opened Brae during a hot summer and at a time when many new breweries were opening up in our region and beyond. It seemed appropriate to our desire of being a recognisably Australian restaurant to be pouring our guests a cold beer when they came over. The result that I was hoping for from this gesture definitely occurred. Many of our guests, particularly those who live close by (farmers) or in other rural areas and may not be inclined to venture to a 'city' restaurant due to their inhibitions about overly formal situations, felt immediately relaxed and, more importantly for the kitchen, open to the idea of any propositions on the menu – like trust or friendship.

But beer requires quite specific foods – those with a good mix of salt, crunch, more salt, umami, a bit more salt and a little sweet. And, again, I want the first few things you eat at Brae to be along the lines of what I like to eat for a relaxed, informal meal with friends – something obviously delicious, familiar and suited to whatever we're drinking.

Both the pretzels and the crisps achieve that – delicious things to crunch before the meal proper and while you finish your beer.

Burnt pretzel, treacle and pork

For 4 people

Pretzels
250g plain (all-purpose) flour
65ml water
8g fresh yeast
65ml milk
20g butter
7.5g squid ink
12.5g dark malt extract

Pork skin crumb
250g pork skin
salt, to taste

To finish
black treacle, for brushing

For the pretzels
Mix 100g of the flour with the water and yeast in a bowl. Cover the bowl with clingfilm (plastic wrap) or a lid and leave it in a warm spot (about 25°C/77°F) for around 3 hours until all foamy and bubbly.

Heat the milk just until it is hot enough to melt the butter, then pour it over the butter in a bowl and add the squid ink and malt extract. Leave the mixture to cool to room temperature, then add it to the yeast-and-water mixture. Add the remaining flour, then knead for 10 minutes until the dough is elastic. Put the dough into a clean bowl and cover it with clingfilm, or put it into a sealed plastic food bag, and leave to prove until doubled in size.

Knock back the dough, then chill it.

Take approximately 8g dough and roll it out evenly like a grissini, rolling your hands outwards, away from each other as if using a rolling pin, until you have a straight pretzel that is the same width and shape as a pencil but is about 20cm long. Place the strip on a Silpat on a baking sheet. Repeat with the remaining dough.

For the pork skin crumb
Seal the pork skin in a pan or on a plancha until it is blistered and caramelized, and all the fat has rendered away. Scrape off any unrendered fat so just the crisp skin is left. Freeze the skin. Once frozen, process it in a Thermomix until it resembles a fine golden crumb. Season with salt and reserve until needed, either frozen or in an airtight container.

To bake
Preheat the oven to 180°C (365°F).

Bake the pretzels for 12–15 minutes until just crisp.

With a pastry brush, brush the pretzels with treacle and place back on the baking sheet. Once they are all brushed, bake for a further 2 minutes until the treacle is caramelized and foaming. Working quickly, put the pretzels into the pork skin crumb and coat them completely. Leave to cool to room temperature before serving.

Salt and vinegar crisps

For 4 people

Crisps
2 potatoes – it is best to use potatoes that are not only tasty but visually striking. We use two varieties, Crimson Pearl and Midnight Pure, that have been developed by a local potato breeder based in the Otway ranges
sunflower oil, for deep frying

Seasonings
freeze-dried sherry vinegar powder
sea salt

Peel the potatoes and slice them finely on a mandoline.

Heat the oil in a deep-fat fryer to 140°C (285°F). Carefully drop the potato slices into the hot oil and fry until crisp, moving them around regularly with a slotted spoon or similar utensil so that they fry evenly.

Once cooked, drain the crisps thoroughly on absorbent paper, removing any excess oil, and season them with both the vinegar powder and salt.

As a snack, allow 2–4 crisps from each type of potato per serve. Arrange the crisps in small bowls so that they are laid out in alternating colours. Serve with a beer.

Hapuku and crisp skin

For 4 people

Hapuku
1 fillet, weighing around 700g, is
more than sufficient but, to
ensure freshness and quality it
is best to use whole fish around
2.5kg
rock salt or coarse sea salt, to cover
2 litres milk
few sprigs of thyme
10 black peppercorns
olive oil

Crisp skin
skin from 1 hapuku or snapper
olive oil
salt

Fish stock
cleaned head and bones from the
hapuku (see above) or snapper
bones

Mackerel stock
2kg slimy mackerel
olive oil

Parsley oil
75g parsley leaves
salt
200ml olive oil
5g garlic

Fish mayonnaise
200ml fish stock (see above)
300g mackerel stock (see above)
3g agar-agar
16g gold leaf gelatine, hydrated
200ml olive oil
15ml parsley oil
salt, to taste

To finish
freeze-dried mandarin
12 fennel sprigs
12 chive tips and flowers

For the hapuku
Fillet the fish. You'll need 1 fillet for this
recipe – use any further flesh for other
preparations. Reserve the cleaned head
and bones for the stock, and the skin for
making the crisp skin.

Sprinkle rock salt over a tray that is of
an adequate size to fit the hapuku fillet
comfortably and lay the fillet on the tray
with the skin-side facing down. Cover
the flesh of the fish liberally with salt and
refrigerate for 72 hours.

After the salting time has elapsed, rinse
away any excess salt from the fish and
completely submerge the fillet in water
to refresh it. Leave it, refrigerated, for
72 hours submerged in water – it is
important to change the water every
12 hours to adequately remove the salt.

Once refreshed, place the hapuku
carefully in a wide-based saucepan
and cover with the milk, thyme and
peppercorns.
Set the pan over a low heat and bring the
milk to a gentle simmer, ensuring it never
boils hard. Once at boiling point, turn off
the heat and allow the milk and fish to
cool to room temperature.

Lift the hapuku from the milk and flake
it into bite-sized pieces. Reserve in olive
oil, refrigerated, until needed.

For the crisp skin
Scrape all fat and flesh from the fish skin,
then lay out the skin in a dehydrator.
Dehydrate at 60°C (140°F) for 8–12 hours.
Once dried, cut the skin into 4cm pieces
(they will puff up to double this size when
fried). Fry the pieces, one by one, in olive
oil at 220°C (428°F), using 2 pairs of long
tweezers to shape the puffing skins into a
rough rectangle – not too perfect so as to
appear over-handled. Drain on absorbent
paper and season to taste.

For the fish stock
Cover the fish head and bones with water
and simmer for around 2 hours, skimming
any impurities as they rise. Strain carefully
and chill the stock immediately.

For the mackerel stock
Preheat the oven to 160°C (320°F).

Using scissors, remove the fin, tail and
wings from the fish. Rub olive oil over the
mackerel and place them on a baking tray.
Roast the mackerel until they have an even
golden appearance.

Once the desired colour is achieved,
transfer the fish to a stockpot, taking care
not to break them. Add enough water to
cover the fish. Simmer the stock for around
2–3 hours until the liquid is deep golden
in colour and has a rich roasted fish flavour.
Strain the stock through a fine sieve
(strainer), then chill it immediately.

For the parsley oil
Blanch the parsley in salted boiling water,
then refresh it in an ice slurry. Squeeze out
any excess water, then combine the parsley
with the olive oil and garlic in a Thermomix,
processing at 50°C (122°F) for 10 minutes.

Once processed, transfer the oil to a fine
sieve (strainer) lined with cloth set over
a bowl and let the cloth hang overnight
until the oil has strained through it. Reserve
the strained oil, covered and refrigerated,
until needed.

For the fish mayonnaise
Combine the fish stock and mackerel stock
in a saucepan with the agar-agar and heat
gently to 92°C (198°F). Add the bloomed
gelatine and transfer the liquid to a
Thermomix. Process the mixture on a high
speed setting whilst streaming in first the
olive oil, then the parsley oil. Keep
processing until the temperature drops
to 50°C (122°F).

Place the resulting emulsion in a tray and
leave to set hard in a refrigerator. Once set,
return the mixture to the Thermomix and
process on a high speed setting until the
texture of mayonnaise is achieved. Season
to taste with salt and reserve at room
temperature. Note that, due to the gelatine
content, this mixture will set hard each
time it is refrigerated and will need to be
puréed before each use.

To serve
Coat the hapuku pieces in mayonnaise and
place a piece on each piece of crisp skin.
Using a Microplane, shave freeze-dried
mandarin over the fish, then scatter over
the fennel and chives and flowers.

Recipes

Chilled broth of broad bean, green almond and strawberry, fig leaf and yogurt whey

When you work closely with a garden, spend time in it daily and allow yourself to be open to its suggestive nature, there are surprises at every turn that can lead to some spectacular ideas for dishes. Some can be magical and far more intellectual and cohesive than most cooks could ever hope to imagine or create. Of course, the ability to be sensitive and non-judgemental about possibilities is important, and finding the right binding agent to bring seemingly disparate ingredients together will always be left to us as cooks.

I'm amazed at how long an idea for a dish can float around in my subconscious. It's rarely words that I think in, rather flashes of flavours and aromas that meld together with memories and the desire to create. These can take their toll, as more and more ideas roll in without any logical translation coming out, and of course many of these ideas never manifest into anything at all, but just remain as baggage, reminding me over and over again for years that I should work on certain 'what if's.

Whenever I hit a creative flatline, which is often, I make my way to the garden to see if I can respond to whatever is there. I'm hoping to find something that sparks a dialogue between myself and nature. I move through the garden, breaking off or cutting things to taste, digging around in the dirt, smelling plants and allowing myself to be open to appreciating the energy that a healthy garden on a healthy piece of land can give off.

Occasionally, something happens that is far better than I could have hoped for, although, as it's happened a few times now, I believe I'm subconsciously looking for it, like a buzz. Certain ingredients are simply in season and growing together close by, and by some type of luck, I eat them in a sequence that allows the flavours to meld as they do on your palate when you eat something you consider to be a perfect dish. And you get a such a shock as you realize you've discovered something you had never previously imagined and have never seen, and certainly haven't eaten in your life. At that moment, a whole, completed idea, from start to finish, goes click. It just happens. And instead of trying to complicate anything, which invariably blankets some of the raw energy that exists in something that is so precisely of a moment, you just collect what you need and put those things together as a dish somewhere in the menu that day, even if just for one service. This recipe is a perfect example of this.

Chilled broth of broad bean, green almond and strawberry, fig leaf and yogurt whey

For 4 people

Fig oil
125g young fig leaves
1 litre olive oil

Yogurt whey
10g tender young fig leaves from
  trees just prior to fruiting
200ml whey extracted from
  hanging sheep's milk yogurt

Broad beans
400g baby broad (fava) beans
salt

Almonds
20 peeled tender or
  green almonds
solution of 1 litre water
  to 1g ascorbic acid

Strawberries
Mix of around 40 small Japanese
  and wild strawberries, both
  traditional red and fraises de
  bois white

Flowers
Coriander flowers

For the fig oil
Combine the fig leaves and oil in a vacuum pack and heat at 60°C (140°F) for 3 hours. Leave the resulting oil to infuse for a minimum of 3 weeks before use.

For the yogurt whey
Crush and tear the fig leaves and vacuum seal them with the whey. Leave in the refrigerator to infuse for 12 hours. Strain out the fig leaves and transfer the infused whey to the freezer and freeze until it is icy but not frozen as a solid mass – this will take roughly 30 minutes, but keep an eye on it.

For the broad beans
Remove the broad (fava) beans from their pods and blanch them quickly in salted boiling water. Refresh them and then remove the second skin. Keep the beans covered with a damp cloth to avoid them oxidizing and drying out.

For the almonds
Peel the almonds to reveal the inner jelly-like tender almonds and place these in the water/ascorbic acid solution. It is best to peel the almonds as close as possible to the time of service.

For the strawberries
Clean any dirt from the strawberries.

For the flowers
Cut the flowers from the stems using sharp scissors and wash them quickly in chilled water. Store them on a damp cloth in a sealed container until needed.

To serve
Dress the double-podded baby broad beans and the strawberries with a little of the fig oil and season with salt. Make a pile of these in the centre of each serving bowl and arrange the tender almonds amongst them. Pour over a spoonful of the yogurt whey, adding any frozen pieces to the top of the other ingredients. Arrange flowers on top and drizzle with more oil.

Ice plant and dried sake

For 4 people

4–8 large budding ice plant tips
  with the tender stem
lemon-pressed olive oil
salt, to taste
lemon zest
freeze-dried sake

Dress the ice plant in the olive oil as if you were dressing salad leaves, then season with salt as if seasoning a salad. Microplane lemon zest over the top, then sprinkle liberally with freeze-dried sake.

Iced oyster

It's a funny thing, the way texture, or the inability to cope with a particular texture, can completely ruin someone's chance of enjoying a flavour they'd probably like.

Oysters, for me, are the best representation there is of the flavour and aroma of the sea. A good oyster from southern Australia in winter or early spring, while the Southern Ocean is still at its coldest, can transport me to a lifetime of memories of swimming in the ocean and being knocked under by crashing waves, or driving along the Great Ocean Road in winter with the car windows open, or breathing in the sea mist while walking along the rocks down around Apollo Bay. As a cook, for any dish where I want to encapsulate the feeling of being by or in the sea, oysters, or at least their juice, are usually the go-to ingredient.

Unfortunately, even in a restaurant where most of our guests are open to new food experiences and generally put themselves in the hands of the kitchen, oysters still polarize. And it's not their flavour, because the fact is, I've never met anyone who doesn't like the smell of the ocean – particularly a cold ocean at its freshest. It's the texture that seems to be the trouble for some people.

This has played on my mind for a while. For quite some time many people have commented on how textural my food is. With a confident grasp of texture and the way in which we tend to use various dried ingredients to season others, I've incorporated oysters (or the flavour of the sea) into many dishes, from lamb, beef and wallaby to kale, broccoli and asparagus. Usually it goes unnoticed as it's not mentioned on menu descriptions, and the resulting umami or pleasant savouriness and crunch is enough to stop anyone who has an aversion to oysters bothering to ask. However, it has been difficult to write oyster on a menu and get those who start to panic when they see the word to relax. But spending time at the beach in both summer and in winter with my daughter, Ivy, started me thinking down a path.

For many years, even before we started going to the beach with Ivy, I've always had an ice cream or a milk shake when at the beach. And not just in summer, because we spend a lot of time on the Great Ocean Road in winter too. I had family holidays here in winter, and Jules and I often came here when the weather was pretty average. There's something very special about the south west coast of Victoria in winter – the sea is powerful, with big swells, so it's just a raw, energized and natural place to spend time. As Ivy has grown up we've continued the tradition, and often going to the beach, which is only 25 minutes' drive from Brae, is really just an excuse to get an ice cream.

Earlier this year I was thinking about the oyster texture thing and my own habit of eating ice cream by the sea, and I thought we should try combining those two things. My reasoning, at the end of the day, was almost too simple – everyone likes the sea (at least, the freshness of the aroma of a cold sea) and everyone likes ice cream. I thought the sugar content that's usually in an ice cream base would be an issue, but when an oyster is on point it's also sweet – it has a saltiness, sure, but there's a sweetness too, just as there is in a clean ocean.

Surprisingly, this concept didn't take many tweaks, and for a dish that's so simple in its creation, it really has been one of the most popular things we've done at Brae. The ice cream base is milk, but with the addition of brine taken from the oysters when shucked. The meat is dehydrated and ground to a powder, as is sea lettuce – these are both sprinkled over the ice cream. And then the acid to bring back some of the sweetness is freeze-dried sherry vinegar powder – a reworking of a fairly traditional seasoning for oysters.

The presentation helps play the game – the guests don't know what they're going to eat and those who are not from the oyster school are generally convinced by our service staff, who tell them how much they'll enjoy it. As most guests eat the iced oyster for the first time we often see a look of confusion on their faces; it's usually the thought 'but hang on, I like ice cream' that gets them over the line.

Iced oyster

Oyster powder and oyster water
2 dozen Pacific oysters, such as
    Coffin Bay

Oyster ice cream
(for 1 Pacojet canister)
25g caster sugar
1.5g sorbet neutral emulsifier/
    stabilizer
115ml cultured milk
115ml full-fat (whole) milk
150ml oyster water (see above)
30g milk powder
70g dextrose
35g trimoline

Sea lettuce powder
30g sea lettuce (add more if you
    find the blades of your food
    processor will not cut such
    a small amount)

Seasonings
oyster powder (see above)
sea lettuce powder
freeze-dried sherry vinegar powder

For the oyster powder and oyster water

Shuck the oysters, saving not only the meat but also the shells and all the water from inside the shells. Pass the water through a fine sieve (strainer), removing any shell and grit. Reserve 150g of the water, refrigerated, for making the oyster ice cream. Wash the shells thoroughly and store in the freezer.

Lay the oysters on absorbent paper to remove any excess liquid, then transfer them to a dehydrator and dry them at 60°C (140°F) for around 12 hours or until completely dry.

Grind the dried oysters to a fine powder in a food processor, then sift away any large pieces. Store the powder in an airtight container.

For the oyster ice cream

To achieve ice cream of the correct texture, it is important to ensure each ingredient is added to the ice cream base when it reaches the stipulated temperatures.

Take 10 per cent of the caster sugar, combine it with the neutral stabilizer and set aside.

In a wide-based saucepan, combine the milks and reserved oyster water and whisk so they are combined. Gently heat the mixture to 25°C (77°F) and add the milk powder, stirring constantly so that it does not fall to the bottom of the pan. Continue warming the mixture to 35°C (95°F) and add the rest of the caster sugar, the dextrose and trimoline. Continue to heat the mixture to 40°C (104°F), then add the neutral stabilizer/sugar mix. Continue to heat the ice cream base gently, whilst stirring constantly, until it reaches a temperature of 85°C (185°F). Then remove the saucepan from the heat and emulsify the ice cream base with a stick blender. Place the finished base in a container and refrigerate overnight or for at least 12 hours.

The following day, re-emulsify the mixture, strain it through a fine chinois, then place it in a Pacojet canister and freeze it to −28°C (−18°F). Pacotize and churn this ice cream at least twice before serving.

For the sea lettuce powder

Wash the harvested sea lettuce in salted water, picking through it carefully to ensure all sand, shells and other debris are completely removed. It is important to wash the sea lettuce many times, and to give it a good soak in abundant water, as it holds a lot of grit.

Once the sea lettuce is completely free of any impurities, it is a good idea to taste it to check for salt content. If it is too salty, give it a quick soak in fresh water until the desired salt level is achieved.

To dry the sea lettuce, place it in a dehydrator and dry it at 55°C (131°F) for 6–12 hours. Process the dried sea lettuce in a food processor to a fine powder. It will hydrate readily, so this powder must be stored in an airtight container.

To serve

Churn the ice cream so that it is quite soft and easy to work with.

Sprinkle a little of each of the sea lettuce and oyster powders on the inside of each reserved shell and fill the shells, one by one, with oyster ice cream, smoothing the tops with a spatula. Return the shells to the freezer and leave them to freeze to a firm eating texture.

When ready to serve, sprinkle each oyster with more oyster powder and a little bit of freeze-dried vinegar powder, then completely cover the ice cream with sea lettuce powder so that it appears as if each one is completely green.

Lemon cucumber and lemon myrtle

For 4 people

Pickling liquor
130g caster sugar
200ml Chardonnay vinegar
60ml lemon juice
40ml lime juice
500ml water

Cucumber
1 large or 2 small lemon
  cucumbers (other types of
  cucumber will work in this
  recipe also)
salt

Spice mix
lemon myrtle powder
Davidson plum powder
Sansho pepper leaf powder

For the pickling liquor
Dissolve the sugar in the vinegar and citrus
juices and add water. Due to the amount
of acidic liquids, this mixture generally
does not need to be heated to dissolve
the sugar but, if by chance, everything is
combined and the sugar is not dissolved,
simply warm it slightly and stir the
sugar until it has dissolved completely
in the liquid.

For the cucumber
Peel the cucumber(s), taking care not to
take off too much flesh. Place in a stainless
steel bowl. Sprinkle liberally with salt and
leave to stand for approximately 1 hour.
This helps to remove some of the moisture
from the cucumber and also seasons it.
  After the salting time has elapsed, rinse
away the excess salt, dry the cucumber
and place it in a vacuum pack with the
pickling liquor. Compress the pickle into
the cucumber several times. Allow the
cucumber to sit in the pickle under vacuum
for a minimum of 3 hours prior to service.

For the spice mix
Combine the powders at a ratio of 4 parts
lemon myrtle to 2 parts Davidson plum
and 1 part sansho. Reserve the mixture
in an airtight container.

To serve
Remove the cucumber from the pickle and
slice them in half lengthways and then into
10cm pieces that are slightly different from
each other, allowing 2 pieces per serve.
Sprinkle the powder mixture across the
cut sides and serve.
  To really utilise the refreshing palate-
cleansing quality of these cucumbers,
they are best served quite cold.

Radish and oyster cream

For 4 people

Pickling liquor
250ml water
65g caster sugar
30ml lemon juice
20ml lime juice
100ml Chardonnay vinegar
Note – this recipe yields enough
to pickle around 30 radishes

Radishes
8 radishes – either French
  Breakfast, Cherry Belle, Red
  Meat or Flamboyant varieties
pickling liquor (see above)

Oyster cream
100ml cultured cream
100ml cream
15ml oyster water
1g sea lettuce powder
(see page 82)
1g oyster powder (see page 104)
5g finely chopped fennel fronds
salt, to taste
Note – this recipe yields enough
for around 20 portions

To serve
olive oil

For the pickling liquor
Warm the water and dissolve the sugar
in it. Add the citrus juices and vinegar
and leave to cool.

For the radishes
Wash the radishes, ensuring all hidden dirt
around the stems and leaves is removed.
Place the radishes with the pickling liquor
in a vacuum pack and compress several
times. Allow the radishes to sit in the pickle
under vacuum for a minimum of 1 hour.

For the oyster cream
Combine all the ingredients, except the
salt, and whisk gently to a very soft peak.
The cultured cream can overwhip very
easily and quickly turn to butter, so
take care. Check the seasoning and
reserve, covered, in the refrigerator
until needed.

To serve
Place a spoonful of the oyster cream to
one side of each serving plate. Dress the
leaves and stems of the radishes with olive
oil and lay them down alongside the oyster
cream. The radishes can be dipped in
the cream.

Recipes

Prawn, nasturtium, finger lime

It's always seemed a bit silly to me to peel a prawn. The big ones, sure, but the shells on the smaller ones are certainly edible and the heads contain so much flavour. If I'm eating prawns at Christmas with my family (which is sort of a tradition in Australia), I'll just pop the whole thing in, enjoying the crunch and the flush of head juices.

At Brae, we peel them, to give our guests a chance to enjoy a very pure version of the flavour and texture of the prawn tails, but I also want them to enjoy the intensity of what's inside the head, so we serve the heads barbecued and dressed in a garlic vinaigrette or a refrito that I learnt in the Basque country. It's basically garlic, parsley, oil and cider vinegar and is used liberally there on seafood cooked 'a la brasa'. If you eat at any of the famous fish restaurants in Getaria you'll eat this type of vinaigrette, used to baste various types of seafood over and over again while they slowly roast over txakoli vines.

I'm surprised though at how many people have never eaten or at least sucked on a prawn head. Prawns are surely the most iconic crustacean in Australia and there are many varieties all around the coast – I've almost felt compelled to force them into the arena with this dish, and to not give our guests the chance to discard them as they usually might. Here there's a reversal of the norm. We serve the meat raw but take the time to cook well what many would consider to be the waste – nose to tail isn't just about hooved beasts.

Inside the parcels is a mix of cultures, but for most Australians, they are familiar ingredients. Tamarind and fish sauce play with tomato and lemon-infused olive oil and, each day, when this mix is prepared before service and brought to me for tasting, I get to think about the way our multiculturalism influences and informs us as cooks and as people. When the chef de partie with Thai genes in his family seasons the mix, it's heavy with fish sauce and balanced with the sour note of tamarind, but if the Anglo-Australian chef that grew up eating Italian food in Melbourne seasons it, it can taste like a marinara. Both are right.

We place the parcels made with the tail meat with jewel-like finger lime on top, near the barbecued heads, hinting that they were once attached, and ask the customers to suck out the brains and then eat the parcels.

Prawn, nasturtium, finger lime

For 4 people

Tomato paste
5kg heirloom tomatoes
75g tamarind paste
7g salt
Note – these quantities yield
more paste than is required for
this recipe

Prawns
approximately 4 sashimi-grade
  prawns
15g shallots, very finely chopped
30g tomato paste (see above)
1g sea salt
2.4g anchovy-based fish sauce
1g chopped chives
grated lime zest and juice, to taste

Nasturtium
4 large nasturtium leaves, each
  at least 10–15cm wide
salt, to taste

Vinaigrette
1 garlic clove
100ml olive oil
10ml apple cider vinegar
chopped parsley, to taste

Finger lime
1 finger lime, with red flesh
  squeezed out

For the tomato paste
Juice the tomatoes and remove any seeds. Transfer the tomato juice to a saucepan and slowly cook down to 750g until a rich paste is achieved. Season with the tamarind paste and salt and refrigerate until needed. Any amount that is unused will store well in vacuum for around 2 weeks or can be frozen.

For the prawns
Remove the heads and shells from the prawns and devein the meat. Keep the heads on absorbent paper, taking care not to break the legs or antennae – these will be grilled later.

You will need 75g prawn meat. Halve each prawn lengthways and cut the meat into an even small dice.

Blanch the shallots in boiling water for around 10 seconds. Strain and, when cool, add to the prawn meat, along with the other ingredients. Check the seasoning and add lime zest and juice to balance the seasoning if necessary. Reserve, refrigerated, until service.

For the nasturtium
Blanch the nasturtium leaves in salted water for approximately 5 seconds so they are just wilted. Refresh in iced water and lay them out to dry on absorbent paper.

For the vinaigrette
Chop the garlic super-finely, then combine it with the remaining ingredients, but add the parsley just before serving or the acid in the vinegar will oxidize it and turn it an off-green to brown colour.

To finish
Prepare a barbecue.

Fill each of the nasturtium leaves with 15g of the prawn mix, folding each leaf neatly into a parcel, and leaving the stem still attached to the leaf on the outside. Place a little of the finger lime on top, then arrange on a plate with even distances between the parcels and the rest of the plate. Dress the prawn heads in the vinaigrette and grill them quickly over charcoal, basting them with more vinaigrette as they cook. Cook them to medium-rare so that the juices inside do not coagulate but are slightly cooked and do not taste raw. Season the prawn heads with salt to taste and place them between the parcels on the plate. It should appear that each head belongs to a parcel (its tail).

Potato and eel sandwich

For 4 people

Eel
1 shortfin eel, smoked over
  Australian hardwood, such as
  river red gum, skinned and boned
1 litre milk
150–200g young Nicola
  or Dutch cream potatoes
salt
olive oil

Potatoes
sunflower oil, for deep frying
2 potatoes – use potatoes that are
  not only tasty but visually striking,
  such as Crimson Pearl
  or Midnight Pure
salt

To finish
finely sliced chives

For the eel
Given that the eel will have migrated from the sea into an estuary and matured in river water, it doesn't hurt to purge it for 12 hours or so in milk to remove a little of the excessive muddy flavour. It's worthwhile checking the flavour first to see if it's OK – and, if not, submerge the skinned and boned fillets in milk and leave, refrigerated, for 12 hours.

Once purged, remove the eel fillets from the milk and drain on absorbent paper, patting them dry. Purée the eel in a food processor. Once the meat is broken down to a paste, pass it through a tamis to remove any fine bones and reserve it at room temperature in a sealed bowl.

Peel the potatoes, cut them into even-sized pieces and boil them in salted water until tender. Once cooked, strain the potatoes and sit them in the colander over the pan in which they were cooked to steam dry. When dry but still warm, pass them through a ricer or mouli and combine the resulting potato purée with the eel at a ratio of 2 (eel):1 (potato). Check the seasoning, then transfer to a piping (pastry) bag.

For the potatoes
Heat the oil in a deep-fat fryer to 140°C (285°F).

Peel the potatoes and slice them finely on a mandoline. Carefully drop them into hot oil and fry until crisp, moving them around regularly with a spider or something similar so that they fry evenly.
Once cooked, transfer the potato slices to absorbent paper to drain and dry thoroughly. Season with salt. Reserve 2 slices of potato per sandwich.

To finish
To make each sandwich, pipe a little of the eel mixture onto a slice of potato and sandwich it with another slice that is similar in size. Place some chives on top.

Potato and eel sandwich; Brook trout and nut butter crisp (recipe overleaf)

Brook trout and nut butter crisp

Nut butter
(for 1 Pacojet canister or
   around 600g)
100g parsley leaves
80g nasturtium leaves
20g rocket (arugula)
40g dill
35g fennel fronds
20g turnip leaves
20g radish leaves
100g macadamia nuts
100g pine nuts
75g pistachio nuts
50ml water
10g salt

Fish crisp
skin from 1 hapuku or snapper
olive oil
salt

To finish
50g brook trout roe
freeze-dried mandarin
mixed spring/summer flowers

For the nut butter
Blanch the leaves and herbs in boiling
water very briefly, then refresh them
in iced water.
   When cold, squeeze out all the water.
Combine the leaves and herbs with the
remaining ingredients. Freeze rapidly in
a Pacojet canister until the temperature
reduces to −18°C (0°F). Once frozen,
process in the Pacojet several times,
freezing in between each processing
if necessary, until a smooth nut butter
is achieved. Store in the refrigerator.

For the crisp skin
Scrape all fat and flesh from the fish skin,
then lay out the skin in a dehydrator.
Dehydrate at 60°C (140°F) for 8–12 hours.
Once dried, cut the skin into 4cm pieces
(they will puff up to double this size when
fried). Fry the pieces, one by one, in olive
oil at 220°C (428°F), using 2 pairs of long
tweezers to shape the puffing skins into a
rough rectangle – not too perfect so as to
appear over-handled. Drain on absorbent
paper and season to taste.

To finish
Spread a little nut butter over the fish crisp,
cover with roe, then Microplane over some
freeze-fried mandarin. Cover with mixed
fragrant flowers and serve.

Raw pea and lemon aspen tart

For 4 people

Peas
40g raw sugar snap peas
   (10g per tart)
extra virgin black sesame oil
grated lemon zest
salt, to taste

Lemon aspen cream
37.5g caster sugar
62.5ml water
250g lemon aspen
37.5g butter
12.5ml lemon juice
2g agar-agar
0.5 gold leaf gelatine, hydrated
salt, to taste

Kelp purée
kombu reserved from dashi (see
   page 200)
100ml water
sea salt, to taste

Sea lettuce shortcrust
285g plain (all-purpose) flour
10g sea lettuce powder
   (see page 82)
227g chilled butter
58ml iced water
3g sea salt
Note – these quantities yield
enough pastry to make
20 small tartlets

Leaves per serve
3 leaves each of Moroccan
mint, peppermint and black
Mitcham mint

For the peas
Shell the sugar snaps and sort through them, reserving only the smallest peas. Season them liberally with the black sesame oil and Microplaned lemon zest and season with salt. Separate the dressed peas into 10g portions.

For the lemon aspen cream
Make a simple syrup with the sugar and water.

Gently sauté the fruit in the butter and syrup, simmering gently until the fruit softens. Pass the fruit and liquid through a tamis to remove the seeds and then through a finer sieve (strainer). Stir in the lemon juice.

Add the agar-agar to 200g of the lemon aspen water. Heat the mixture slowly to 90°C (194°F). Add the hydrated gelatine, transfer the mixture to the refrigerator and leave to set hard. Process the set lemon aspen gel to a fine cream, season to taste, and transfer to a piping (pastry) bag.

For the kelp purée
Combine the reserved kombu from dashi with the water and place the mixture in a vacuum pack. Braise the kombu at 80°C (176°F) for 12 hours. Once broken down and soft, purée to a smooth paste. Season with sea salt and reserve in a sealed container.

For the sea lettuce shortcrust
Combine 120g of the flour with the sea lettuce and butter and beat in a stand mixer on a medium speed setting. Stop the mixer and add the remaining flour, along with the iced water and salt. Restart and mix until a dough forms and comes off the side of the bowl.

Divide the dough into 2 pieces, wrap in clingfilm (plastic wrap) and leave to rest, refrigerated, for a few hours.

Once fully relaxed, remove the pastry and roll out the pieces between parchment to a thickness of 3–4mm. Cut out 6cm rounds with a pastry cutter, returning the pastry to the refrigerator to cool down if it warms up too much at any time.

Line 4 × 6cm non-stick tart moulds with the pastry and freeze.

Preheat the oven to 170°C (338°F).

Once the raw tarts are frozen, bake them for 12 minutes or until cooked but not overly coloured. Remove the cooked tart shells from the moulds and leave to cool to room temperature.

To serve
Place a little of the kelp purée in the centre of each tart shell and then circle it with lemon aspen cream, ensuring that the edges of the tart cases remain clean and higher than the purées. Fill the tops of the tarts with the peas and finish with the mint leaves. Serve at room temperature.

Sea urchin and chicory bread pudding

Sea urchin
4–8 sea urchin 'tongues',
    depending on size

Chicory bread pudding
15g chicory root powder
70ml full-fat (whole) milk
butter, for greasing
135ml cream
37.5g egg yolk
87.5g whole wheat (wholemeal)
    sourdough bread

To finish
grated lime zest

For the sea urchin
Victorian sea urchin begin their season in the depths of winter, from around the start of August and can be found up and down the west coast, starting in Williamstown on the edge of Melbourne all the way to South West coast of Australia.

If using whole sea urchin, use protective gloves to handle the urchin and good butchers' scissors to open the shells. Using long tweezers or a wooden spoon, remove the roe carefully and rinse in a light dashi (see page 200 for a recipe for Simple Dashi) if needed. Reserve the sea urchin, refrigerated, until needed – but as with all seafood served raw – ensure that the roe is at room temperature at the time of service.

For the chicory bread pudding
Put the chicory root powder into a heat-proof bowl. Bring 55g of the milk to the boil and pour the boiling milk over the dried chicory root to seal it. Leave to infuse for 20 minutes.

Preheat the oven to 140°C (285°F). Butter an oven-proof bread tin (pan) or appropriately sized gastronorm pan.

Once infused, strain off the chicory powder and then top up the liquid using the remaining fresh milk so that there is still 55ml milk. Add the cream, then transfer the mixture to a saucepan and scald it, before whisking it into the egg yolk in the same way as you would if making a custard.

Slice the bread into 5-mm thick slices and lay it in the prepared tin, ensuring the slices are overlapping and that the tin is filled 2–3 slices deep. Pour over the chicory custard mixture, cover with baking paper and kitchen (aluminum) foil and bake for 1 hour.

Once the baking time has elapsed, leave the pudding to cool to room temperature, then press it with a light weight and transfer to the refrigerator to chill. When the pudding is quite cold and firm, cut out rounds from the pudding that are wide enough to support the sea urchin – roughly 2cm.

To finish
Warm the bread pudding a little to room temperature, so that the custard that has been soaked up by the bread starts to loosen a little.

Place 4 rounds of the bread pudding on a serving plate. Lay the urchin on top of the bread pudding and grate a little lime zest over the top.

Sheep's curd and spring harvest honey grilled with squash blossom over juniper

For 10 balls

Curd
100g sheep's yogurt

Honeycomb
125g caster sugar
63g glucose
30g spring-harvested pure honey
25ml water
7g bicarbonate of soda
  (baking soda)

Leek ash
2 medium-sized leeks, such as
  Jaune du Poitou or King Richard
olive oil
Note – these quantities yield more
leek ash than is required for this
recipe, but this is the minimum
amount that can be processed
when dry

Curd balls and to serve
juniper branches, cut to roughly
  15cm lengths, for smoking
reserved curd (see method)
3g leek ash (see above)
8g honeycomb (see above)
2g Davidson plum powder
salt, to taste
4 squash blossoms with around
  5cm of stem still attached

For the curd

To dry the curd, place the sheep's yogurt into ricotta baskets or a sieve (strainer) lined with absorbent cloth and leave to hang over a bowl for around 48–72 hours. Once the whey has drained away, the resulting curd will be dry and have an increased intensity of flavour. Reserve the curd to make the curd balls.

For the honeycomb

Combine all the ingredients, except the bicarbonate of soda (baking soda), in a saucepan and heat to a caramel. When it reaches 153°C (307°F), quickly sift in the bicarbonate of soda and whisk the caramel as it bubbles. Pour out the resulting honeycomb onto a Silpat and leave to cool and harden.

Once hard, freeze the honeycomb and, when frozen, process it to a fine powder in a food processor. Keep frozen until needed.

For the leek ash

Prepare a barbecue.

Remove the outer leaves from the leeks and dress them in olive oil. Lightly grill them over charcoal, then leave them to dry overnight using the residual heat left in a masonry oven. (Alternatively, dehydrate them at 55°C (131°F) for around 24 hours, or until completely dry.)

The following morning, process the leeks to a fine powder in a food processor. Reserve in an airtight container.

For the curd balls and to serve

Prepare a barbecue, adding juniper branches for smoking.

Combine the curd, leek ash, honeycomb and Davidson plum powder well and add salt if required. Roll the mixture into equal-sized balls with a diameter of roughly 2.5cm, to fit inside the blossom. Stuff 1 ball into each of the squash blossom. Ensure the blossoms have plenty of stem left on so that they look a little like lollipops. Quickly grill on the barbecue over the smoking juniper branches.

Serve the blossoms alongside smoking juniper branches.

Smoked eel doughnut and brook trout roe

For 4 people

Smoked eel brandade
125g Dutch Cream potatoes
225g smoked shortfin eel paste
  (filleted, soaked, pureed and
  passed to make a paste)

Choux
120ml milk
65g butter
100g sifted plain (all-purpose) flour
2 eggs

To finish
sunflower oil, for deep-frying
salt, to taste
brook trout roe

For the smoked eel brandade
Boil the potatoes as you would for a potato purée, ensuring they are well cooked and steamed dry before going through the ricer.
Combine the eel paste and potato purée so that you have what is, essentially, an eel brandade. Cover and keep in a warm place.

For the choux
Combine the milk and butter in a saucepan and bring to the boil, then add in the flour in one go, stirring continually over a medium heat until the mixture comes away from the side of the pan and is cooked.
Transfer the batter to a stand mixer and beat on a low setting, dropping in the eggs one at a time. Add the brandade and continue to beat until combined.
Store the doughnut batter at room temperature in a piping (pastry) bag fitted with a star nozzle.

To finish
Heat the oil to 170°C (338°F).
Pipe 10–12cm lengths of doughnut batter into the hot oil and fry for around 1½ minutes on each side or until golden and crisp. Transfer the doughnuts onto absorbent paper to remove any excess oil and season with salt as needed.
Cover 1 side between the ridges with brook trout roe.

Turnip and brook trout roe

For 4 people

Turnip
16 small Japanese or golden
  turnips
100g unsalted butter
20ml shiro (white) soy sauce
approximately 100ml water
50g brook trout roe

Turnip leaf cream
150g turnip leaves
37.5ml cultured cream

For the turnip
Clean the turnips, removing the leaves, stems and any dirt, reserving the leaves for the leaf cream. Place them in a small saucepan with the butter, soy sauce and water and bring to a gentle simmer. Cover the pan with a lid and reduce the emulsion, at the same time cooking the turnips to al dente and glazing them in the butter and soy.

Once cooked, remove the turnips from the cooking liquor and cut off their tops, making a little hollow in each turnip. Fill the hollows with the brook trout roe.

For the turnip leaf cream
Blanch the leaves from the turnips in seasoned, boiling water, removing them when cooked but before their chlorophyll begins to fade. Squeeze out any excess water and then combine the blanched leaves with the cultured cream and process.

Combine the blanched turnip leaf and cultured cream and process in a Thermomix for 5 minutes on a high speed setting at 50°C (122°F).

To serve
Spoon a little of the turnip leaf cream onto each serving plate. Place 4 turnips on top of the leaf cream on each plate.

Wallaby and flax, wattle and lemon myrtle

For 4 people

Salted dandelion
250ml water
40g salt
125g wild dandelion buds
  or dandelion 'capers'
Note – these quantities yield
enough for about 30 portions, but
this is a minimum quantity to make

Flaxseed crisp
160g flaxseed (linseed)
300ml water
2g salt
Note – these quantities yield
enough to make around 45
portions

Nettle butter
100g stinging nettle leaves
50g parsley
200g butter, at room temperature
salt, to taste

Wallaby
100g wallaby fillet
ground wattle seed
ground lemon myrtle
ground mountain pepper
salt, to taste
mustard oil

To serve
16-20 sheep sorrel leaves

For the salted dandelion
Bring the water and salt to a boil, then pour it over the dandelion buds, discarding any that open up. Cover or seal them in the brine in a vacuum pack for a minimum of 4 days and a maximum of around 1 month.

For the flaxseed crisp
Combine the flaxseed and water, add the salt and leave to hydrate for around 6–8 hours. Flaxseed has a natural gelling agent that appears like mucus or endosperm around the hydrated seed. Once this is well developed and the seeds are fully hydrated, spread the flax thinly on a Silpat and leave in a warm place for about 3 hours to dry.
   Break the dried flax crisp into bite-sized pieces and reserve in an airtight container.

For the nettle butter
Blanch the nettle and parsley quickly in salted boiling water – this will bring the chlorophyll to the surface of the leaves. Refresh in iced water, then squeeze out any excess water so as to not dilute the flavour and consistency of the finished butter.
   Combine the leaves with the softened butter in a food processor and purée until a homogenous green butter is achieved. Season to taste with salt and store refrigerated.

For the wallaby
Remove any sinew from the meat and dice it into a fine mince that is suitable in size and texture for eating raw. Season to taste with the remaining ingredients and use the mustard oil to provide heat and moisture. As this element of the dish will be consumed raw, it is imperative to work quickly and hygienically and keep the wallaby cold at all times. Once seasoned and if not serving immediately, cover the wallaby with clingfilm (plastic wrap) and reserve, refrigerated, until it is needed.

To serve
Spread a little nettle butter on each of the flax wafer pieces. Top with the raw wallaby. Place 3–5 dandelion buds, depending on the size on the wafer, on top, then scatter over some sheep sorrel.

Brae farm honeycomb seasoned with beetroot and brook trout roe

For 4 people

Honeycomb
4 pieces of honeycomb

Beetroot and onion broth
2kg large brown onions
1kg beetroots (beets)
olive oil
egg white
xanthan gum
salt
Japanese brown rice vinegar

To finish
1 kaffir lime leaf
salt, to taste
4 large dessertspoonfuls
  of brook trout roe
dried sansho powder
approximately 6 black sesame
  seeds per serve
4 green coriander seeds (pick the
  green coriander seeds from
  flowering coriander late in its
  season when the seeds have not
  yet hardened)
4 coriander flowers with a little
stem attached

For the honeycomb
Cut each piece of honeycomb down to roughly 5cm × 2cm, removing the outer layer of wax and exposing the honey.

For the beetroot and onion broth
Preheat the oven to 140°C (285°F). Prepare a barbecue.

Slice the onions in half through the skins and across the core.

Wrap the beetroots (beets) in kitchen (aluminum) foil and bake for 1 hour.

Rub the cut side of the onions with a small amount of oil. Place the onions, cut-side down, on a plancha and cook until blackened. Once black, transfer the onions to a barbecue. Set them slightly above the heat and allow the water inside the onions to boil. At the same time, remove the beetroot from the foil, place them low against the charcoal and blacken the skins.

When the water begins to bubble out of the onions, transfer them to a stainless steel bowl and cover with clingfilm (plastic wrap). Leave them to steam in the bowl.

Remove the blackened beetroots from the barbecue and rub the black skins away. Leave to cool.

Preheat the oven to 70°C (158°F).

Remove the cooled onions from the bowl and, with the back of a paring knife, remove all traces of carbon. This step is important as any blackness will result in a bitter stock. Remove the skins and put the cleaned onions, along with the charred beetroot, in a stainless steel bowl, wrap the bowl tightly with clingfilm and transfer to the oven. Bake for 12 hours, leaving the onions and beetroot to steam slowly and their sugars to caramelize.

Once the baking time has elapsed, remove the onions and beetroots from the oven and push them several times through a juicer, extracting as much juice as possible. Then pass the juice through a fine sieve (strainer).

Mix the egg white with the juice at a ratio of 100g egg white to 1 litre juice. Put the mixture into a vacuum pack sealed without vacuum.

Set a steam oven to 100°C (212°F). Transfer the vacuum pack to the steam oven and cook for around 2 hours. (You can place the sealed bag into a pan of boiling water and boil it hard for the same period of time – just be careful the pan does not boil dry.) The protein in the egg white will set during this period and clarify the liquid. Once the albumen is set and patches of clear liquid appear, remove the liquid from the bag and strain it through a fine sieve (strainer). Thicken the broth with xanthan gum at a ratio of 4g xanthan gum to 1litre of liquid. Season and add vinegar to taste, then keep refrigerated. For this recipe the broth is served at room temperature.

To finish
Blanch the lime leaf briefly in boiling water – 5 seconds will be just long enough to take away the rawness and to make the texture more palatable. Refresh the leaf in iced water. Slice it into long, super-fine strips.

Warm the honeycomb slightly under a salamander or grill (broiler) so that the honey and comb is softened. Season with a little salt to balance the sweetness.

Place 1 piece of honeycomb in each serving bowl and pour a little of the beetroot and onion broth around. Spoon over the roe, letting some fall into the broth. Delicately season the roe in each serving with sansho powder, sesame seeds, a coriander seed and a coriander flower.

Blood and pistachio, rhubarb and preserved blackberry

Makes 18 × 17g biscuits

Rhubarb stock syrup
500g rhubarb
1 litre water
250g caster sugar

Rhubarb pieces
300g rhubarb
50g caster sugar
400ml rhubarb stock syrup
  (see above)

Blackberry preserve
250g blackberries
80g caster sugar
2g pectin
125ml water
10ml lemon juice

Blood and pistachio biscuits
50g fresh pork blood
120g caster sugar
110g ground almonds
90g ground pistachios
4g finely chopped pistachio per
  biscuit, to coat
icing (confectioners') sugar, to dust

For the rhubarb stock syrup
Roughly chop the rhubarb and combine it with the water and sugar in a vacuum pack. Steam for 20 minutes. Remove the ingredients from the vacuum bag, strain away the solids and chill the liquid.

For the rhubarb pieces
Peel the rhubarb and place it in a saucepan with the sugar sprinkled evenly over the top. Leave to stand for 30 minutes or so, then gently warm the pan, dissolving the sugar and steaming the rhubarb to al dente.
Remove the rhubarb and leave it to cool. Deglaze the pan with the rhubarb stock syrup and reduce it to 100ml. Reserve the rhubarb glaze in a piping (pastry) bag. Cut the rhubarb into even 1.5cm pieces that will fill the centre of the biscuits.

For the blackberry preserve
Combine all the ingredients in a saucepan and cook to 108°C (226°F). Process to a fine purée and leave to cool and set. Reserve in a piping (pastry) bag.

For the biscuits
Preheat an oven to 170°C (338°F).
Combine the blood, caster sugar and ground nuts and process together to form a paste. Roll the mixture into 17g balls, coat with the finely chopped pistachio and then shape them into small biscuits, about 2.5cm across. Make a little indentation in the top of each biscuit and fill each of these with first with a little blackberry preserve, then a piece of rhubarb.
Bake the biscuits for exactly 13 minutes. Remove the biscuits, dust them with icing sugar and then dab a little rhubarb stock syrup over each piece of the rhubarb. Leave to cool.

Recipes

Knives, forks, spoons and plates

The bulk of any menu at Brae falls into this category – the second act, or the savoury and sweet plated dishes. Here you'll eat vegetables, fish and seafood, game and dry-aged meats, lots of liquids, dressings and different seasonings made by drying out various edibles, then frozen things and sweeter things, maybe even things not commonly served as a dessert. It's where you'll eat the most volume of food and you'll get to use cutlery, even eat off your own plate.

I guess we tend to follow a fairly traditional progression in this section of the menu – but only because it resonates with how I like to eat and it makes sense. We start with often complex dishes that are light in palate weight, with a fineness of flavour, then move through to richer, ballsier dishes, using more animal fats, barbecued ingredients and heavier proteins. We don't value any of these plates less or more than those they follow or proceed, and we don't follow any guidelines for what size they should be either – yes, we portion to standardise cooking times, but we approach plate sizes simply based on how we feel a particular item would best be enjoyed when eaten in the scheme of all the other things you will eat in a menu at Brae, and with generosity always being a consideration. Crayfish, sea urchin, pork jowl, aged older beef, sun-warmed strawberries – things that are generally not eaten every day by our guests – are served in volumes to be enjoyed rather than as just a token.

I don't necessarily see the menu as a list of dishes but more like a puzzle or web that fits together, with each dish relating to those around it and each day's menu speaking with a common voice.

Aged Pekin duck wood roasted on the bone, quandong and dried liver

There are some dishes that come onto menus on a whim and are gone just as quickly. Because of our connection to the garden they are often vegetable-based and appear as different ingredients come into season together, cooked simply and just laid on a plate, sometimes with seasonings of seafood or meat, and inserted into a menu simply to complement the moment and reflect the day or week.

Other dishes are more complex and spend time hanging around, hitting their peak over and over again as they are refined and played with, and as we become proficient with certain techniques.

This dish of aged duck has quite a profound significance for me as it really toes the line with the type of food I want to serve. It is something with an identity that is unique to this part of Australia, handled in a way that is true to our endeavours of showcasing the best possible version of a product, and it is cooked in a way that is technical but honest and grounded rather than fussy or tricky, with complementary flavours reflecting our location.

The ducks, Pekin in breed, are from Great Ocean Ducks, a small-scale property just inland from Port Campbell, at the end of the Great Ocean Road that's owned by a local family. The birds are raised ethically and sustainably, with the health of the property and also the owners in mind, and in harmony with the seasons and surrounding land. They are free ranging on pasture, fed a diet of fruit (strawberries in summer/pears and apples at other times) and selected grains. Then they are dry-aged by us, until they reduce in moisture and reach the flavour profile that we prefer, which takes somewhere between 14 and 21 days, depending on the weight of the bird and time of the year. To cook, they are stuffed with rye grass hay cut from our paddocks, then roasted with the residual heat left in the brick oven after the bread has been baked – a conscious decision to maximize, rather than waste, the heat stored in the masonry.

Mead, fermented from Brae farm honey, is used to soak nasturtium flowers and stems before they are barbecued. This is a technique I wanted to use for a while – to take something as delicate as a flower and place it over a heat that, for the most part, is considered only for robust proteins or larger vegetables, and if handled badly, would just destroy the petals. But it is done with such care and attention that the resulting product provides a nice contradiction to many people's expectations of grilling over fire. The quandong, an Australian fruit, grown further west in Victoria, just north of the Grampians (and also in South Australia), is tart and textural and perfect against smoke and fat, and seems a logical partner for duck cooked in this way in Australia. And then the liver, fried slowly, chopped and dried, and mixed with cocoa and lime zest, provides another rich layer to the dish.

Aged Pekin duck wood roasted on the bone, quandong and dried liver

For 4 people

Mead
5kg raw honey
15 litres rainwater, at room
    temperature

Duck
1 Pekin duck, approximately 2.4kg,
    pasture-raised and fruit-finished,
    aged for around 14 days
Note – this recipe uses the crown
only, but the legs and necks can
be used for other dishes
olive oil
salt
hay from rye grass

Duck glaze
500ml soft red wine
250ml orange juice
125g raw honey
1 star anise
5 peppercorns
10g coriander seeds
5g fennel seeds

Duck sauce
125g caster sugar
25g liquid glucose
1.5 litres brown chicken stock
Japanese brown rice vinegar

Rhubarb stock syrup
500g rhubarb
250g caster sugar
1 litre water

Quandongs
50g quandongs, halved and stoned
100ml rhubarb stock syrup
    (see above)
Cabernet Sauvignon red wine
    vinegar

Dried liver
150g chicken livers
250ml water
250ml milk
2.5g salt
anchovy fish sauce
500ml sunflower oil
20g cocoa nibs, finely shaved
    with a Microplane
10g lime zest

Nasturtium flowers
12 nasturtium flowers, long
    stems attached
mead (see above)

For the mead
Combine the honey and rainwater in
a sterilised fermenting vessel, stirring
vigorously in one direction to create
a downward vortex. While the liquid is
still moving, stir against the momentum
of the vortex until the honey is combined
with the water. Do this every day until
fermentation begins and then for a further
7–10 days. Once fermentation has slowed
a little, leave undisturbed, fitted with an
airlock, to continue to ferment for up to
3 months or until the fermentation has
subsided. The mead is now ready for use
but can be bottled at this stage for further
development. Keep in a cool place.

For the duck
Our supplier generally delivers the ducks
already plucked, so preparing them is
usually just a case of ensuring all plumes
have been removed. If they are difficult
to remove at the time they arrive at the
restaurant, they tend to become looser
as the ducks age. At worst, they can be
removed once the ducks are cooked. This
recipe uses the crowns only, so remove
the legs and thighs, necks and wishbones.
Clean up the crowns, then leave in
a dry-aging area for around 14 days.

For the duck glaze
Reduce the red wine by half, ensuring
the alcohol is burnt off. Add the remaining
ingredients and continue to reduce the
liquid to a thick syrup consistency,
resulting in around 250ml.

For the duck sauce
Combine the sugar and glucose in a dry
pan and heat to a deep golden caramel
colour. Deglaze with the brown chicken
stock and reduce to around 750ml.
Add the rice vinegar to taste just before
service – usually just 2ml per portion.

For the rhubarb stock syrup
Peel the rhubarb, reserving the peelings.
Chop the rhubarb roughly. Dissolve the
sugar in the water, then pour into a
vacuum pack along with the rhubarb
pieces and peelings – the addition of the
skins gives the stock a deep red colour.
Steam for 20 minutes. Leave to cool,
then strain and reserve the liquid.

For the quandongs
Cut the quandongs into quarters and
combine them with the rhubarb stock
syrup. Vacuum pack and cook at 60°C
(140°F) for 30 minutes. Refresh in iced
water, and once chilled, strain the liquid
from the quandongs into a pan and reduce
it by half. Season with a splash of vinegar,
then return the quandongs to the pan.

For the dried liver
To clean the livers, remove any sinew, outer
membrane and fat and make a small cut in
each end. Vacuum pack with the water,
milk and salt and poach in a water bath for
3 hours at 40°C (104°F). Strain the livers,
dry them and then marinate for 30 minutes
in the fish sauce at a ratio of 20 per cent
fish sauce per weight of liver.
    Remove the livers from the marinade and
pat them dry. Place them in a saucepan
with the sunflower oil and gently heat to
140°C (285°F). Hold this temperature for
around 15 minutes or until the livers are
completely cooked and slightly dehydrated,
but not fried.
    Remove the livers from the oil, pat them
dry of any excess oil and pulse them in
a food processor until torn into a floss.
Combine 100g liver floss with the finely
shaved cocoa nibs and lime zest. Store
in an airtight container.

For the nasturtium flowers
Prepare a barbecue.
    Soak the flowers in mead for at least
1 hour. Remove them and lay over the
barbecue until the flowers have wilted
slightly and the mead has caramelised
a little. The stems should have slight
char marks and will have a delicate
smoked flavour. →

To finish

Paint the duck crown with the glaze, rub some olive oil into the skin and season well with salt. Leave to come to room temperature prior to roasting. Stuff the cavity with hay. Lay the duck on a rack in a roasting tin and place it in a masonry oven once it's cooled to 200°C (390°F) at the front. Generally, a 1.6kg crown will take around 30 minutes to roast to medium-rare. Rotate the duck if necessary and inspect it every 10 minutes or so, checking the widest part of the breast next to the wing joint for doneness. If using a conventional oven, set the temperature to 160°C (325°F) and start checking for doneness after 25 minutes.

When roasted, remove the hay from the cavity, reserving it to smoke the duck. Let the duck rest for 10 minutes or so, and then place the hay over charcoal until smoking heavily. Position the duck over the smoke, ensuring that it is far away from the heat, so it doesn't continue cooking. Smoke the crown for 3–5 minutes. This short burst imparts a little of the smoking hay flavour onto the skin of the duck – it does not really penetrate the meat.

Warm the quandongs in their liquid. Warm the nasturtium flowers. Bring the duck sauce to temperature.

Place 4–5 quarters of quandong and a little of their reduced poaching liquid in the centre of each serving plate. Lay 3 flowers to the right of the quandongs and a spoonful of liver/cocoa floss at about 11 o'clock.

Carve the duck breast off the bone and then again across the fillet into the desired serving size. Season the flesh well with salt, place a portion of duck onto each plate below the quandongs and dress with the sauce.

Blue mackerel lightly cured with apple and nasturtium

Green juice
0.25g ascorbic acid
75g Granny Smith apple
37.5g nasturtium leaves
   and stems
12.5g radish leaves
12.5g wild cabbage leaves
salt, to taste

Blue mackerel
2 blue mackerel, each weighing
   around 300–400g
sea salt

To finish
4 × 2mm thick slices of Granny
   Smith or similar high-acid apple,
   cut in to battons (around 5 per
   serving)
16–20 strips of blanched celtuce
   stem (4–5 per serving)
approximately 40 thinly sliced
   rounds of mixed radishes,
   including black and watermelon
   (approximately 10 per serving)
20–30 small nasturtium leaves
   with stem (6–8 per serving)
olive oil

For the green juice

Place the ascorbic acid into the vessel that will catch the juice. Combine the apple with all the leaves and juice them through a vegetable juicer. Strain out any solids. Chill the juice as quickly as possible, to help avoid oxidisation. Season with a little salt as needed and reserve, refrigerated, until required. This juice oxidises in both colour and flavour quickly, so needs to be made close to when needed. Separate some juice and reserve this to dress the plates.

For the blue mackerel

Head, gut and fillet each mackerel, separating both sides down the pin-bone line into fillets. The belly fillets are occasionally smaller, so the best portions come from the top loin.

Sprinkle sea salt liberally over a tray and lay the fillets skin-side down on the tray for a brief semi-cure. Sprinkle salt on the flesh of each fillet as well, with the intention of seasoning and firming rather than drying out the fish. This salt will not be washed away and no further seasoning will be required, so it's best to perform the salting process no more than 2 hours prior to serving. Once they have been salted, place the mackerel fillets to marinate in the green juice for around 1 hour, refrigerated.

To finish

Bring the mackerel to room temperature, then remove the fillets from the green juice. Arrange 2 fillets on each plate. Spoon over some of the reserved green juice so that there's quite a bit on the plate. Dress the apple, celtuce, radishes and nasturtium with a little olive oil, then scatter them over the mackerel, allowing them to fall onto the plate. Add some olive oil to the fish, and to split the juice, then serve.

Blue mackerel and air dried pork, lemon, walnut and cauliflower

For 4 people

Fermented tomatillo juice
Makes enough to fill a 2-litre jar
2 flowering heads of dill
8 horseradish leaves
approximately 20–25 golf-ball
    sized (or slightly larger) tomatillos
brine solution at 2.5g salt to
    100ml water

Fermented cucumber skin powder
2 large cucumbers
sea salt

Blue mackerel
2 blue mackerel, weighing
    approximately 300–400g each
sea salt, to cure

Pork fat
1 piece of cured pork back fat,
    weighing approximately 100g
salt, to taste

Whole lemon purée
2 large lemons (approximately
    350g total weight)
150ml soy milk
4.5g gellan gum
salt, to taste

Walnuts
approximately 12 walnuts, recently
    harvested, shelled and peeled

Cauliflower
½ cauliflower, cut into 2 large
    pieces

For the fermented tomatillo juice
Sterilize a jar and pack in the aromatics. Tightly pack in the tomatillos, then cover with a salt solution at room temperature, made with 2.5g salt to 100ml water, using enough of the solution to cover the contents of the jar completely. Seal the jars and leave at room temperature for at least 3 weeks to ferment.

Prepare a barbecue. Remove the tomatillos, pat them dry and chargrill them so that they are blistered but not cooked. Transfer them directly to a juicer, extract their juice, then chill the juice quickly so that it does not oxidize. Store the juice in a sealed container, refrigerated, until needed.

For the fermented cucumber skin powder
This recipe provides a good way of utilising the skins of cucmbers if you are eating them regularly in the summer. Peel the cucumbers and toss the skins with 2.5 per cent of their weight in sea salt. Transfer to a vacuum pack and leave at room temperature for around 10 days to ferment. Once fermented, transfer the skins to a dehydrator and dehydrate at 55°C (131°F) until completely dry. Process the skins to a powder with either a spice grinder or a mortar and pestle and reserve in an airtight container until required.

For the blue mackerel
Head, gut and fillet the mackerel, separating both sides of each fish down the pin-bone line and into fillets. The belly fillets are occasionally smaller, so the best portions come from the top loin. Sprinkle salt liberally over a tray, lay the fillets skin-side down on the tray, then sprinkle salt on the flesh of each fillet as well, with the intention of seasoning and firming rather than drying out the fish. Transfer to the refrigerator and leave the fish to semi-cure. This salt will not be washed away and no further seasoning will be required, so it's best to perform the salting process no more than 2 hours prior to serving.

For the pork fat
Slice the cured back fat into thin rectangular slices using a meat slicer – aim for slices that measure roughly 7cm × 12.5cm. Store the slices between sheets of greaseproof (wax) paper.

For the whole lemon purée
Juice the lemons, reserving the rinds and the juice. Cover the juiced-out rinds with water in a saucepan and cook down until the water has all but evaporated. Combine the cooked lemon rinds with the soy milk and gellan gum in a Thermomix and process on a high setting to 95°C (203°F). Transfer the purée to a bowl and leave it in the refrigerator for at least 3 hours to set. Then return the set mixture to a food processor and process on a high speed setting until a thick purée is achieved. Season to taste with salt and stir in around 50ml of the reserved lemon juice, which brings back some of the freshness to the purée. Reserve in a piping (pastry) bag.

For the walnuts
Split the peeled walnuts in half so that you have a flat surface to work with. Shave them finely using a mandoline or truffle slicer. It's best not to handle the walnut pieces too much once shaved as this breaks and compacts the pieces. With this in mind, place the sliced walnuts straight onto a serving spoon.

To finish
Pat dry the skin of the fish on absorbent paper or towel. Rub a little olive oil on the skins before sealing the fillets skin side-down on a plancha, taking care not to cook the flesh of the fish.

Marinate the sealed fish in the tomatillo juice for around 1 hour.

Season the pork fat slices and warm them so that the fat becomes translucent. You need to do this very quickly under a salamander or heat lamp so they don't begin to fry.

Place each fillet of mackerel on a serving plate and cover it by draping a piece of lardo over the top. Sprinkle a good pinch of fermented cucumber skin powder over the lardo and scatter over 2.5g shaved walnuts per serving. Shave the cauliflower over the top using a Microplane grater, then sprinkle over another pinch of cucumber powder. Squeeze a little lemon purée opposite the fish and serve.

Barbecued wallaby, not barbecued

For a long time I wasn't much of a fan of cooking or eating wallaby, which is probably due to trying it years ago, overcooked and with incompatable accompaniments – but I felt a bit guilty about it, because as Australians, whether it be recent immigrants or original settlers, we probably have a responsibility to eat more native non-introduced foods. Raw wallaby, on the other hand, is texturally delicious – soft, with a delicate gaminess. Bennett's wallabies, wild shot on Flinders Island, feed on the rich saltgrass pastures the island is renowned for and, with no predators, they have flourished. Their meat is healthy, it's lean, low in fat and quite high in protein and minerals, with a real flavour of its habitat.

From an environmentally sustainable point of view, wallabies find themselves at the top of the food chain. They have the ability to negate methane production through an enzyme found in their digestive system and so do not contribute to methane gas emissions the way that other livestock in Australia does (which results in around 10 per cent of Australia's total annual greenhouse gas emissions), require around 70–90 per cent less water per kilo of edible meat than traditionally eaten meats such as beef and lamb, and so are much more suited to our dry continent. And with their soft paws, rather than the hard hooves found on ruminants, they live far more harmoniously in the Australian environment, without contributing to erosion and compacting of the land.

With this dish I want our guests to experience the texture and pleasure of eating raw wallaby, without the fuss that's often made by some about eating raw meat, so I introduced all the familiar and comforting flavours of the barbecue, flavours that are intrinsically associated with meat-eating in Australia and that reference the way wallaby has been consumed for thousands of years – cooked over fire and eaten in the hand.

There is a much more subtle intent with the presentation of this dish, too. There's the similarity to picking up and dipping a hand roll – something completely commonplace for even the most Anglo Australians, and from observing our guests we've found that this act introduces an element of reassurance to eating a meat that, to many, even though it's indigenous, is unfamiliar.

Barbecued wallaby, not barbecued

For 4 people

Wallaby
75g wallaby fillet
3ml mustard oil
3ml anchovy water
5.6ml shiro (white) soy sauce
0.8g ground wattle seed
0.3g ground native or mountain
  pepper
0.2g ground lemon myrtle leaf
  salt, to taste
20g puffed wild rice

Radicchio
Radicchio brine:
150g raw honey
200ml water
4 large radicchio leaves

Barbecued beetroot purée
100g Bull's Blood beetroot
  (beets) or other dark beetroot
olive oil
27.5ml soy milk
7ml Cabernet Sauvignon vinegar
7ml smoked olive oil

For the wallaby
Remove any sinew from the wallaby fillet
and dice the meat finely, as you would
for tartare. Fold through the remaining
ingredients, except the puffed wild rice,
just prior to serving and season with
salt to taste.

For the radicchio
First make the brine. Combine the honey
with the water and heat gently to dissolve
the honey. Wash the radicchio leaves, place
them in the brine and leave for around
6 hours.
  Prepare a barbecue. Remove the leaves
from the brine and, without drying them
too much (to avoid removing the honey),
place them on an extremely hot chargrill
and grill the leaves a little, charring
the edges.

For the barbecued beetroot purée
Preheat the oven to 140°C (285°F).
Wrap the whole beetroots (beets) in
kitchen (aluminum) foil and bake for
around 1 hour. Dress the baked beets with
olive oil and place them on the chargrill,
which should be positioned low down, next
to the charcoal. Leave the beets to become
quite coloured, almost black. Once charred,
combine them with the other ingredients
and process using the high speed setting
on a food processor until a thick purée
is achieved. Pass through a fine sieve
(strainer), then put the barbecued beetroot
purée into a piping (pastry) bag and reserve.

To finish
Combine the wallaby tartare with the
puffed wild rice at a ratio of 2:1. Divide the
mixture into 4 portions and place 1 portion
inside each of the charred radicchio leaves,
then roll up to resemble a spring roll.
  Pipe a little of the barbecued beetroot
purée at the left of each serving plate
as a thick dipping sauce and then place
a wallaby roll to the right of it.

Pork

For a very long time, pork farming was pretty average in Australia, with pigs held in low regard and typically bred and raised indoors in dark sheds. The resulting pork was of a low and probably quite unhealthy quality and, at the same time, we lived with strange government 'health' guidelines encouraging the public to eat only 'lean' cuts of pork – and to overcook them.

Naturally free ranging and foraging pigs are, unfortunately, a relatively new concept in Australian agriculture but, on the plus side, we're now seeing some amazing-quality pork, with ethical pig farming becoming more common.

I've worked with the same pork producer for a number of years now. I returned from Spain – where I was obviously exposed to pork farmed with, and held in, the highest regard – around the same time that Anthony and Amanda Kumnick returned from living abroad and started a pig farm at their property, Greenvale Farm in Western Victoria. Seven years down the track, I think they produce some of the best pork in Australia and I feel lucky to have the privilege of working with them and their product.

Raising heritage breeds, including Tamworth, Duroc, Berkshire and even some breeds that have become extinct in their place of origin, like the Wessex Saddleback, Greenvale Farm currently raises around 1,700 pigs from around sixty breeding sows – a steady rise from the dozen or so I remember when we first met. These traditional breeds grow at a slower rate than those favoured by industrial agriculture, and as a result, have more time to develop muscular strength, health and flavour.

The pigs are raised without growth hormones, being left to grow in their own time, and without antibiotics, being medicated only when and if required for their health. Whilst they are free to range and feed on grass as is their inclination (which, in turn, helps to keep their levels of aggression and agitation down), they are also fed a grain-based diet that comes from pastures and supplementary grain feeding. The 1,000 or more acres that is Greenvale Farm is currently being moved towards a closed system, whereby the farm will not only produce all replacement stock (which it already does) but also grow and produce all the feed that the pigs need for their biodynamic diet.

Pork, in various textures, features on most menus at Brae, and over time, we've become quite skilled at identifying the right breed of pig for our requirements. Of course, using as much of the beast as possible is important, and with pork of this quality, we find it's easy to find uses for random bits and pieces. But, more so, rather than working with a pig-is-a-pig-is-a-pig mentality, we now use specific breeds for their particular benefits. Wessex Saddlebacks have a great mid-section and so are used for their belly, back fat, racks and loins, while Berkshires have incredible intramuscular fat and so the neck, jowl, legs and shoulders are fantastic. Tamworth are great for their fat-to-meat ratio so, again, cuts like the belly have good proportions.

One particular technique we rely on heavily at Brae, which is only possible with exemplary pork, is to render the fat from any trim or sections of the animal that won't be cured, for example, and use it to baste meat while it's on the grill, but also to rest the meat fully submerged in this fat during its resting time immediately after. It's a technique that's become integral to our meat cooking program, and something we've now also extended to some beef cuts when they come off the chargrill (in this case, rested in rendered smoked bone marrow fat). We find that doing this not only provides a fantastic medium for keeping the piece of meat warm and moist in the period between grilling and serving, but also allows us to impart nuances of flavour into the meat – whether it be by slightly smoking the fat or, in some cases, with pork dishes, introducing a sweet and bitter note with a chicory root reduction that's rubbed on the meat and then imparts its flavour into the fat.

Berkshire pork and dandelion

For 4 people

Dandelion root glaze
400ml water
50g dandelion or chicory root
   powder
60g caster sugar

Pork ribs
rack of Berkshire pork ribs
   (allow 1 large rib per person)
olive or sunflower oil
salt, to taste
lime zest

For the dandelion root glaze
Boil the water, then pour it over the dandelion root powder, sealing the dandelion immediately so there is no loss of flavour. Leave to infuse for 10 minutes. Strain the resulting liquid and then discard the solids.

Combine the infusion with the sugar and place the mixture in a saucepan set over a medium heat. Reduce the liquid to approximately 125g. Leave to cool, then check the consistency and flavour – the glaze should be quite sticky, sweet and bitter all at once.

For the pork ribs and to serve
Prepare a barbecue.

Make sure the ribs are neat and tidy, trimming away any flaps of meat or fat that aren't part of the ribs or intercostal section. Rub them with some oil prior to cooking.

Seal the ribs on a plancha, then pat them dry, removing any excess oil.

Paint the glaze all over the ribs, then barbecue them slowly to medium-rare. If they seem dry, it may be necessary to baste the ribs with more glaze as they cook. When done, season with salt and cover liberally with Microplaned lime zest. Slice the ribs to separate them, baste again to ensure they are well coated in the sticky glaze, and serve.

Berkshire pork cooked overnight, shiitake and fermented cabbage

For 4 people

Black garlic
whole heads of garlic

Fermented cabbage
1 large Chinese cabbage (wombok)
sea salt
sunflower oil, for deep frying
Note – this yields more fermented
cabbage than is needed for
this recipe

Pork
1 large pork jowl (cheek)
rendered pork fat
salt, to taste

Pork stock
10kg pork bones with a nice
   covering of meat
10 shallots
approximately 250g rendered
   pork fat
5 litres reduced veal stock
5 litres white chicken stock
2.5 litres water

Pork and smoked eel glaze
15g Japanese white sesame oil
15g rendered pork jowl (cheek) fat
100g shallots
20g ginger
2g red Szechuan pepper
2g mountain pepper
50g maple syrup
100ml sake
400g smoked roasted eel
   (bones and meat)
2.5kg pork stock (see above)

Shiitake
8 large shiitake mushrooms
100ml white chicken stock
salt →

For the black garlic

To ferment the garlic, wrap the heads tightly in several layers of kitchen (aluminum) foil and place into a dehydrator. Dehydrate at 55°C (131°F) for around 5 weeks or until the cloves turn a deep caramelized black colour and have a chewy texture. Separate and peel the cloves. Reserve 2 cloves to slice thinly for this dish and store these in an airtight container or vacuum sealed until needed. Dehydrate the remaining garlic cloves for a further 24–48 hours until hard and bone-dry. Process to a fine powder. Store in an airtight container until needed.

For the cabbage

Separate all the leaves from the cabbage and wash them thoroughly. Pack the leaves tightly into a sterilized preserving jar and cover with brine, made by mixing water with sea salt at a ratio of 100ml to 2.5g. Ensure the brine is at room temperature. Seal the jar tightly. Leave to stand at room temperature for a minimum of 5 days. After this time, remove the leaves and pat dry on absorbent paper. Lay the leaves out on a drying rack and leave to dry until they are almost dry but the stems still retain some moisture.

At this stage, deep-fry the leaves at 140°C (104°F) until the edges of the leaves take on a golden colour. Drain on absorbent paper. Transfer to a dehydrator set at 60°C (140°F) and dehydrate for approximately 3–5 hours or until crisp.

For the pork

Place the jowl in a vacuum pack and cover with the rendered fat. Seal tightly and cook at 80° C (176°F) for 10 hours.

Once cooked, chill the jowl in an ice bath or blast chiller, removing it just before it is completely cooled. While still in the bag, press the jowl with a heavy weight so that it rests flat rather than curled at the edges. Leave to cool completely.

When completely cold, remove the jowl from the vacuum pack, trim off the skin and any excessive amounts of fat and square up the edges.

For the pork stock

Preheat the oven to 180–200°C (400–425°F). Roast the pork bones until coloured a deep golden.

Slice the shallots finely and sweat them in the pork fat until sweet but not coloured. Add the roasted bones, then the liquids to cover. Simmer for around 4 hours, skimming regularly, until the stock is porky and flavoursome. Strain off any solids and reduce the stock to around 5 litres, skimming regularly. Pass the mixture through a fine sieve (strainer) and chill immediately.

For the pork and smoked eel glaze

Warm the sesame oil and pork fat in a wide-based saucepan. Slice the shallots and ginger, then slowly sweat them in the oil and pork fat without colouring. Add the Szechuan and mountain peppers, then the maple syrup and allow to lightly caramelize.

Deglaze the mixture with the sake. Add the eel bones and meat then the pork stock. Bring to a gentle simmer, skimming off any impurities that rise to the surface, and cook out slowly until reduced to 750ml. Pass this through a fine sieve, season and chill rapidly.

For the shiitake

Peel 1 large shiitake per portion, remove the stems and slice each mushroom into even-sized rounds (to a thickness of about 2mm). Combine with the salted chicken stock in a vacuum pack and steam for 30 minutes. Refresh and reserve until needed.

The remaining shiitakes will be served raw. Remove the stems and then slice finely into even slices, allowing 9–10 slices per plate. →

Aubergine and white miso
1 large aubergine (eggplant)
400ml water
15ml light soy sauce
5g caster sugar
4g salt
gellan gum
For the marinade:
1 garlic clove
125g shiro (white miso) paste
60ml light soy sauce
30ml lemon juice
10ml pure or Japanese
  white sesame oil
100ml aubergine (eggplant)
cooking liquor

For the aubergine and white miso
First make the marinade. Mince the garlic and combine it with the miso, soy sauce, lemon juice and sesame oil to form a homogenous paste.

Peel the aubergine (eggplant) and cut the flesh into small pieces. Blanch the aubergine pieces in the water combined with the soy sauce, sugar and salt, keeping it submerged with a cartouche. Simmer for 8–10 minutes to ensure that the aubergine is completely cooked. Once cooked through, remove the aubergine pieces from the cooking liquor. Blend 100ml of the aubergine cooking liquor with the marinade, then combine the aubergine pieces with the marinade at a ratio of 400g blanched aubergine to 100g marinade. Purée the aubergine with the marinade in a food processor, then allow to cool. When completely cold, transfer the aubergine purée to a Thermomix, add gellan gum at a ratio of 0.5g gellan gum to 100g purée and process to thicken the mixture.

To serve
Preheat the oven to 70°C (158°F) and prepare a barbecue.

Warm the pork jowl in the oven for around 20 minutes, then brush it liberally with the pork and eel glaze. Place it on the barbecue and allow the glaze to caramelize while smoking the jowl. Brush the jowl repeatedly with the glaze during barbecuing until it is well coated.

Warm a little of the aubergine purée (you will need roughly 1 tablespoon per serve). Finely slice the black garlic cloves. Place a small spoonful of warmed purée to the right of the centre of each wide serving bowl. Arrange 2–3 slices of the braised shiitake rounds over the purée in each bowl, and add also 2–3 slices of black garlic. Once the jowl is well glazed and has taken on the aroma of the charcoal, season it and cut into even slices. Lay a slice in each bowl next to the other ingredients and cover with 2–3 fermented cabbage leaves and raw sliced shiitake. Dust the black garlic powder through a tea strainer over the top of everything and serve.

Wessex saddleback and fermented roots, barbecued carrot and dried coriander

For 4 people

Fermented roots
1.5kg daikon
1.5kg kohlrabi
1.5kg celeriac (celery root)
Each of the 3 fermenting
jars to contain:
20g coriander seeds
2g lemon myrtle
grated zest of 1 lemon
500ml purified water
20g sea salt
10g dill leaves (left whole
  as a large sprig or two)
Note – these quantities yield more
fermented roots than are required
for this recipe, but as they are
delicious and take time to ferment,
it is best to make them in larger
volumes

Dandelion root glaze
400ml water
50g dandelion or chicory
  root powder
60g caster sugar

Pork
½ rack of pork (4 points/bones)
  from a larger female Wessex
  saddleback
salt, to taste
400g rendered pork fat

Barbecued carrot
150g carrots
olive oil
20ml milk
5ml Japanese brown rice vinegar
5ml smoked olive oil
1.25g gellan gum
salt, to taste
Cabernet Sauvignon vinegar,
  to taste

Dried coriander blossom
coriander flowers, harvested when
  in full flower, just prior to seeding

To serve
20g carrots, peeled and julienned
  salt, to taste

For the fermented roots
Sterilize 3 × 2-litre fermenting vessels so the vegetables can be fermented in separate jars. Put the coriander seeds, lemon myrtle and lemon zest into the jars.
   Prepare the brine for each jar by mixing the water and salt.
   Peel the vegetables, then slice them separately on a meat slicer or mandoline to a thickness of 7mm. Pack the slices tightly into their separate jars and pour over the brine, allowing the liquid to fill any gaps and submerge the vegetables. Place the dill on top, then weigh down any vegetable slices that have risen above the brine with a clean rock or any other fermenting weight and close the lid tightly. Leave the jars at room temperature so that the fermentation begins. After 3 days, remove the dill and let some pressure out of the jars, then reseal the lids and leave for a further 3 weeks. All of the vegetables used here are usually ready at this stage and will keep well for up to 6 months. Once a jar is opened, it should be transferred to the refrigerator.

For the dandelion root glaze
Follow the recipe on page 158 to make the dandelion root glaze.

For the pork
Prepare a barbecue.
   Follow the instructions on page158 to cook the pork.
   Glaze, then barbecue and allow to rest.

For the barbecued carrot
Preheat the oven to 180°C (356°F).
   Wrap the carrots in foil and roast for 1 hour.
   Prepare a barbecue.
   Remove the carrots from the oven, dress with olive oil, then char the carrots over embers until the skins are blackened. Combine 75g of the charred carrot with the milk, rice vinegar, smoked oil and gellan gum and process in a Thermomix on high speed setting to 85°C (185°F). Maintain this temperature for 5 minutes to activate the gellan gum, then transfer the purée to a tray to cool in the refrigerator for at least 3 hours. After this time, process again on a high speed setting. Season with salt and a splash of vinegar to taste. Reserve in a piping (pastry) bag.

For the dried coriander blossom
Trim away the stems from the coriander flowers. Leave to sun-dry or in a warm place. Once dry, process to a powder and reserve in a sealed container until required.

To serve
Julienne equal amounts of the fermented veg, and in the mix also include an equal amount of julienned raw carrot to the julienned fermented vegetables. Allow 5g of each type of vegetable per serve. Check the seasoning but, generally, after the fermentation the vegetables will not require any additional salt. Mix the portions of vegetables together as if it were a coleslaw and place a little to the top right of each serving plate. Dust with a little dried coriander blossom. Below this, pipe around 1 tablespoon barbecued carrot.
   Make sure the pork is well rested but still warm before carving it. Season with salt to taste before plating it with the other ingredients.

Wessex saddleback, onions soured in whey, cauliflower, wild cabbage

For 4 people

Brassica powder
equal quantities of blanched and
    dried brassica leaves, including
    black cabbage, pak choi, red
    Russian kale, nasturtium, or any
    plant from the brassica family
salt, to taste

Dandelion root glaze
400ml water
50g dandelion or chicory
    root powder
60g caster sugar

Pork
½ rack of pork (4 points/bones)
    from a larger female Wessex
    saddleback
salt, to taste
400g rendered pork fat

Soured onions
200g white onions
300g reduced whey – obtained
    from making ricotta, then
    reduced to one-third its original
    weight (see page 220)
salt
apple cider vinegar, to taste

Cauliflower
100g cauliflower
salt, to taste

Wild cabbage juice
80g large French sorrel leaves
20g large nasturtium leaves
    and stems
200g wild cabbage leaves
1g ascorbic acid
salt, to taste

To finish
12 long oxalis leaves

For the brassica powder
Blanch any coarser leaves such as the kales in salted water for around 1 minute and refresh in iced water, ensuring all excess water is squeezed out once cold. The softer leaves can be dried raw.

Dry the leaves in a dehydrator at 55°C (131°F) for around 12 hours or until completely dry. Process the leaves in a food processor on a high speed setting. Sift out any unground pieces through a fine sieve (strainer). Store in an airtight container.

For the dandelion root glaze
Boil the water, then pour it over the dandelion root powder, sealing the dandelion immediately so there is no loss of flavour. Leave to infuse for 10 minutes. Strain the resulting liquid and then discard the solids.

Combine the infusion with the sugar and place the mixture in a saucepan set over a medium heat. Reduce the liquid to approximately 125ml. Leave to cool, then check the consistency and flavour – the glaze should be quite sticky, sweet and bitter all at once.

For the pork
Prepare a barbecue.

Remove the rack/bones from the fillet and tidy up any excessive fat and membranes. Remove the skin. Slice the fillet down the middle so that you have 2 pieces of even length. Seal the meat on a plancha, then brush the meat and the ribs with the dandelion root glaze. Transfer to a barbecue and grill at around 80°C (176°F) until the pork is medium-rare (at 52°C/125°F). Season well, then rest the meat in rendered pork fat at around 40°C (104°F) until the protein is relaxed, about 15 minutes.

For the soured onions
Preheat the oven to 140°C (285°F).

Using a mandoline, slice the onions finely into half rounds. Combine them in a baking dish with the salted reduced whey, cover the dish tightly with both baking paper and kitchen (aluminum) foil and bake for approximately 75 minutes until the onions are just past al dente but not completely broken down. Check the seasoning, then finish with cider vinegar.

For the cauliflower
Slice the cauliflower as finely as possible while still maintaining its shape. Dehydrate at 55°C (131°F) for around 6 hours or until crisp. Check the seasoning. Allow around 10g per serve.

For the wild cabbage juice
Wash the different leaves in abundant water and then pat them dry. Chop the wild cabbage down a little, removing any obviously coarse parts of the stem as these can ruin small electric juicers. Place the ascorbic acid into the vessel that will catch the juice, then juice the leaves over the top, stirring the ascorbic acid through and seasoning with salt as necessary. Cover and refrigerate until needed.

To finish
Warm the onions and place a little on each serving plate, covering it with a good pinch of brassica powder. Place around 10g cauliflower alongside the onions and then dress each plate, around the onions, with the wild cabbage juice. Trim the ribs and carve off 1 rib per serve. Carve the pork to expose the flesh, season well and place 1 rib and a slice of fillet on each plate. Lay a few oxalis leaves over the cabbage juice on each plate and serve.

Hapuku, cured pork and mibuna, fish roe whipped with onion

For 4 people

Hapuku
1 whole hapuku, weighing around
  2.5kg
salt, to taste
olive oil

Pork fat
1 piece of cured pork back fat,
  weighing approximately 100g
salt, to taste

Fermented cucumber skin powder
3 cucumbers
sea salt

Flathead roe cream
200g flathead roe
1 litre water
125g white onions, finely sliced
  and cooked in whey until very soft
300ml reduced whey
25ml cider vinegar
4g gellan gum

Brassica emulsion
100ml water
100g unsalted butter
50g sliced Japanese turnip
1g bonito flakes
25ml shiro (white) soy sauce
salt, to taste

Mibuna stem and juice
about 400g mibuna (leaves
  and stems)
xanthan gum

For the hapuku

Head, gut and fillet each fish, then remove the pin bones. Next, remove the skin, then carefully separate the top loins along the sinew/fillet line into 3 loins. Separate the fillets into 45g portions.

Preheat the oven to 80°C (176°F).

Seal the fish on the side where the skin was, then transfer it to the oven with some moisture in the form of a small oven proof container filled with water, to cook gently – a 40–45g piece of hapuku will take around 8 minutes at this temperature. Once roasted, brush away all the white coagulated protein visible on the surface of the fish, season and brush with olive oil.

For the pork fat

Slice the cured back fat into thin rectangular slices using a meat slicer – aim for slices that measure roughly 7cm × 12cm. Store the slices between sheets of greaseproof (wax) paper.

For the fermented cucumber skin powder

Peel 2 of the cucumbers. Follow the method for making fermented cucumber skin powder on page 142.

Peel the remaining cucumbers. Transfer the skins to a dehydrator and dehydrate at 55°C (131°F) until completely dry. Process the skins to a powder using either a spice grinder or a mortar and pestle. Reserve in an airtight container until required.

For the finished powder, make a mixture of the 2 powders using a ratio of 75 per cent fermented skins powder to 25 per cent dried skins powder. Reserve in an airtight container.

For the flathead roe cream

Follow the instructions on page 182 to make the flathead roe cream.

For the brassica emulsion

Bring the water to a simmer, then whisk the butter into the simmering water and pour the mixture over the turnip slices and bonito flakes. Cover, seal and leave to stand for 1 hour. Strain the mixture and season with the soy and salt.

For the mibuna stems and juice

Separate the mibuna stems and leaves. Reserve 250g of the leaves for juicing.

Cut 50g of the stems into 10–12cm pieces, allowing 4 pieces per plate, depending on their size.

Juice the reserved leaves and pass the juice through a fine sieve (strainer). Thicken the juice with xanthan gum, working with a ratio of 2g xanthan gum per 1 litre juice. Keep the juice chilled to avoid oxidization.

To finish

Allow the pork fat to come to room temperature, then dust it with the cucumber powder and a little salt.

Gently warm the mibuna stems in the brassica emulsion until they are hot but not broken down.

Place a little flathead roe cream on each serving plate, then cover with the mibuna stems and a slice of pork fat. Place the fish next to the other ingredients and spoon the mibuna juice around everything.

Calamari and broccoli, wild greens and blue mackerel

For 4 people

Calamari
2 whole line-caught southern
  calamari, weighing approximately
  600g each

Broccoli
the stem from a large head
  of broccoli
450ml dashi

Mackerel broth
500g whole blue mackerel
olive oil
1 litre purified water

Toasted garlic oil
1 head of garlic
100ml olive oil

Green juice
0.25g ascorbic acid
75g Granny Smith apples
37.5g nasturtium leaves and
  stems
12.5g radish leaves
12.5g wild cabbage leaves
salt, to taste

Greens, per serve
3 Vietnamese mint leaves
a nice mix including at least one of
  each of nasturtium,
  chrysanthemum, brocoli leaf,
  turnip leaf, radish leaf and
  red or green mustard leaf

For the calamari

Lay 1 calamari on a board and, taking care not to break the ink sac, remove the legs and intestine. Remove the ink sac and reserve it for other dishes. Remove the quill, wings and the skin. Using a sharp filleting knife and following the line where the quill was, slice the calamari in half, opening it up to make 1 flat piece. Using the back of a knife, wipe off any impurities that may be inside, taking care not to damage the calamari.

At this stage it is necessary to clean and dry the calamari with a cloth – ensuring that calamari does not come into contact with any water will improve the texture and colour, and give the calamari a longer shelf life. Rubbing it with a cloth, remove any impurities that may be left on the squid and the first membrane of the flesh. Dry the squid and remove the membrane.

Once clean, trim the edges of the calamari, slicing from top to bottom, and portion the calamari into 4 even pieces. Repeat the preparation process with the other calamari.

Stack the calamari pieces and wrap them tightly with clingfilm (plastic wrap). Freeze until hard. Unwrap the calamari and slice it across the shortest edge of the body using a meat slicer, making thin ribbons that resemble noodles. Divide these into 4 × 25g portions. Leave the portions on absorbent paper until required.

For the broccoli

Square up the broccoli stem so that it is rectangular and measures approximately 10cm in length. Using a mandoline, slice the stem lengthways to 5mm, and then cut the slices into even sticks that are about 10cm long and 5mm wide.

Blanch the broccoli sticks in 300ml dashi and refresh in 150ml iced dashi. Remove from the cold dashi and leave to cool, then cut the broccoli into 5mm dice.

For the mackerel broth

Preheat the oven to 160°C (320°F).

Using scissors, remove the fin, tail and wings from the fish. Rub olive oil over the mackerel and place them on a flat roasting tray. Roast the mackerel until they have an evenly golden appearance.

Once the desired colour is achieved, transfer the fish to a stockpot, taking care not to break them. Add the purified water to cover the fish. Simmer the stock for around 2–4 hours until the liquid is deep golden in colour and has a rich roasted fish flavour. Strain the liquid through a fine sieve (strainer), cool immediately and store, vacuum-sealed, until needed.

For the toasted garlic oil

Peel and chop the garlic until it is ultra-fine and almost a paste. Ensure there are no larger pieces. As you chop, occasionally flatten the knife out and spread the garlic across the board to ensure it is all of an even texture. Once the desired texture is achieved, combine the garlic with the olive oil in a saucepan set over a medium heat. Stir constantly, until the moisture evaporates and the garlic turns a toasted golden colour. Then immediately place the base of the pan into an ice slurry and stir the garlic until it is cold. It's imperative that the garlic is cooked far enough but then chilled before overcooking. When cooling the garlic, ensure that no water enters the oil or the garlic will go soft. The end result should be crisp, toasted garlic. Reserve in the oil.

For the green juice

Place the ascorbic acid into the vessel that will catch the juice. Combine all the remaining ingredients, except the salt, and juice them using a vegetable juicer. Strain out the solids and chill the juice as soon as possible to help avoid oxidisation. Season with a little salt as needed and reserve, refrigerated, until required. This juice oxidises in both colour and flavour quickly, so needs to be made as close to serving time as possible.

For the greens

Trim, wash and store the leaves, portioned, until required.

To serve

Transfer the mackerel broth to a saucepan and bring to a boil.

In each serving bowl, place 5g broccoli stem dice, then a portion of the raw calamari over the top. Dress the calamari with the green juice, then pour 100ml boiling broth over the top. Use a spatula or a small spoon to separate the calamari. Top with the greens and drizzle over the garlic oil.

Calamari and fermented celeriac, barbecued peas and beef fat

For 4 people

Fermented celeriac
Makes enough to fill a 2-litre
    preserving jar
20g coriander seeds
2g lemon myrtle leaves
grated zest of 1 lemon
500ml purified water
20g sea salt
3 large celeriacs (celery roots),
    around 700–800g total weight
10g dill leaves (left whole as
    1–2 large sprigs)
Note – these quantities yield more
fermented celeriac than is needed
for this recipe, but as it needs time
to ferment and is delicious, it is
best to make larger volumes

Beef fat
2kg veal shin bones, sliced, or
    200g bone marrow from veal shin

Calamari
1 whole calamari, weighing
400–500g
olive oil

Peas
500g peas in the pod
beef fat (see above)
salt, to taste

Pea juice
Pods and larger peas from the
    peas (see above)
xanthan gum
salt, to taste →

For the fermented celeriac

Sterilize a 2-litre preserving jar and its lid. Put the coriander seeds, lemon myrtle and lemon zest into the jar.

Prepare the brine by mixing the water and salt.

Peel the celeriacs (celery roots), then immediately slice them, using a meat slicer, to a thickness of 7mm. Pack the slices tightly into the jar and pour over the brine, allowing the liquid to fill any gaps and submerge the celeriac. Place the dill on top, then weigh down the celeriac with a rock and close the lid tightly. Leave the jar at room temperature so that the fermentation begins. After 3 days, remove the dill and let some pressure out of the jar, then reseal the lid and leave for a further 3 weeks. The celeriac is usually ready at this stage and keeps well for up to 6 months. Once the jar is opened, it should be transferred to the refrigerator.

For the beef fat

Prepare a barbecue.

You can buy from your butcher 200g marrow that has already been pushed out of the bones. Alternatively, soak 2kg veal shin bones in water for 12–24 hours or until the marrow loosens from the bones. Remove the marrow from the veal shin and purge it in iced water. When super-cold, place 200g of the marrow into a grill basket and cook it quickly (to avoid the fat melting) on the barbecue, allowing it to be heavily smoked over the charcoal.

Once smoked and coloured, put the marrow into a Thermomix and process on high at 70°C (158°F). The resulting liquid will appear to be a dirty oil full of impurities. Place this liquid in a saucepan and bring to the boil, evaporating any water and purifying the beef fat to a clear liquid. Skim and decant through a fine sieve (strainer). Store the beef fat in the refrigerator if making this preparation well ahead of time.

For the calamari

Lay the calamari on a board and, taking care not to break the ink sac, remove the legs and intestine. Remove the ink sac and reserve it for other preparations. Remove the spine, wings and skin. Using a sharp filleting knife and following the line where the spine was, slice the calamari in half, opening it up to make 1 flat piece. Using the back of a knife, wipe off any impurities that may be inside, taking care not to damage the calamari.

At this stage it is necessary to clean and dry the calamari with a cloth – ensuring that calamari does not come into contact with any water will improve the texture and colour, and give the calamari a longer shelf life. Rubbing it with a cloth, remove any impurities that may be left on the squid and the first membrane of the flesh. Dry the squid and remove the membrane.

Cut the calamari into 2 even rectangles measuring approximately 10cm × 12cm and then slice 10-cm strips lengthways from top to bottom with a width of around 7mm.

For the peas

Prepare a barbecue.

Shell the peas, reserving the pods for the juice. Sort the peas, removing any that are too large and reserving those for the juice. Place the smallest, sweetest ones into a grill basket and quickly sauté them over the hot barbecue, drizzling over some beef fat every few seconds. The fat will eventually melt and fall off the peas onto the coals, so the aroma of the smoke will catch the peas. Once cooked, season the peas and chill them quickly over ice.

For the juice

Juice the pea pods and the reserved larger peas 3 times so that all possible juice is extracted. Pass the juice through a fine sieve (strainer), then leave it to stand in the refrigerator for around 1 hour to allow the starch to settle on the bottom. Carefully decant the juice, then thicken it with xanthan gum at a ratio of 3g xanthan gum per 1 litre juice. Season to taste. Reserve the pea juice in the refrigerator until ready to serve. →

Pancetta
50g pancetta

Toasted garlic oil
1 head of garlic
100ml olive oil

Leaves, flowers and herbs,
per serve
3 sheep sorrel leaves
2 Vietnamese mint leaves
3 spearmint leaves
2 lemon balm leaves
5 garlic chives or chive flowers
(season permitting)

To finish
olive oil, for deep frying
salt, to taste
beef fat (see above)
lemon myrtle leaf powder

For the pancetta

Slice the pancetta as finely as possible on a meat slicer, then chop it down to a paste.

For the toasted garlic oil

Peel and chop the garlic down until it is ultra-fine and almost a paste. Ensure there are no larger pieces. As you chop, occasionally flatten the knife out and spread the garlic across the board to ensure it is all of an even texture. Once the desired texture is achieved, combine the garlic with the olive oil in a saucepan set over a medium heat. Stir constantly, until the moisture evaporates and the garlic turns a toasted golden colour. Then immediately place the base of the pot into an ice slurry and stir the garlic until it is cold. It's imperative that the garlic is cooked far enough but then chilled before overcooking. When cooling the garlic, ensure that no water enters the oil or the garlic will go soft. The end result should be crisp, toasted garlic. Reserve in the oil.

For the leaves, flowers and herbs

Trim the stems of the leaves so they all have a clean end, then wash and dry them. Reserve the leaves and flowers on damp paper in a sealed container until service.

To finish

Trim the sheets of celeriac to mimic the size and appearance of the calamari strips.

Heat enough olive oil to submerge the calamari strips to a temperature of 55°C (131°F). Submerge the calamari strips and cook for 5 minutes. Use a slotted spoon to transfer the calamari onto absorbent cloth or paper and season with salt.

Allow 20g calamari strips and about 6 celeriac strips per portion. Combine them so that all the strips are running in the same direction and the calamari and celeriac are bundled together.

In a separate pan, render 20g pancetta paste in beef fat and add 80g peas and a pinch of lemon myrtle leaf powder. When hot, cover with 120g pea juice and check the seasoning, adding not only salt but a little more beef fat if needed.

Divide the pea mixture into 4 portions. Spoon a little from each portion onto the left side of a serving plate. Place the calamari and celeriac on top. Cover with the remaining peas and juice, add a few drops of toasted garlic oil, scatter over the leaves and flowers and serve.

167

Calamari and pickles

For 4 people

Calamari
2 line-caught whole
  southern calamari, each
  weighing about 600g
approximately 250ml olive oil to
  cover the finished portions

Pickling liquor
130g caster sugar
60ml lemon juice
40ml lime juice
200ml Chardonnay vinegar
500ml water

Pickles
2 lemon cucumbers
sea salt
16 cauliflower florets
8 baby Japanese turnips, halved
4 tomatillos, quartered
2 Breakfast radishes, quartered

Egg
2 eggs, each weighing roughly 55g
salt, to taste
mirin, to taste
lemon myrtle leaf powder, to taste

Vegetable juice
300ml daikon juice
180ml fennel juice
100ml cucumber juice
20ml mirin
2g salt
xanthan gum
approximately 2 lovage leaves,
  finely sliced

Leaves per serve
3 rocket (arugula) leaves
2 bower spinach leaves
2 Vietnamese mint leaves
2 lemon balm leaves
2 Black Mitcham mint leaves
2 spearmint leaves

To finish
olive oil
salt, to taste
horseradish

For the calamari
Lay 1 calamari on a board and, taking care not to break the ink sac, remove the legs and intestine. Remove the ink sac and reserve it for other dishes. Remove the quill, wings and the skin. Using a sharp filleting knife and following the line where the quill was, slice the calamari in half, opening it up to make 1 flat piece. Using the back of a knife, wipe off any impurities that may be inside, taking care not to damage the calamari.

At this stage it is necessary to clean and dry the calamari with a cloth – ensuring that calamari does not come into contact with any water will improve the texture and colour, and give the calamari a longer shelf life. Rubbing it with a cloth, remove any impurities that may be left on the squid and the first membrane of the flesh. Dry the squid and remove the membrane.

Once clean, portion the calamari into even 25g rectangular pieces, scoring the inside of each piece with a sharp knife. Place the calamari portions in a dish and cover with the olive oil, ensuring they are completely submerged.

For the pickling liquor
Combine all the ingredients, ensuring the sugar is fully dissolved – if the sugar is added to the citrus juices and vinegar first, the acid usually dissolves the sugar.

For the pickles
Peel and salt the cucumber lightly with a good sea salt, adding a little more salt than you would if you were going to eat the cucumber fresh. Leave it, covered, in a bowl at room temperature for 1 hour. Rinse the cucumber in cold water and cut it into 12–16 pieces with a paring knife (note that you want the pickle vegetables to be the same size). Compress the cucumber pieces in a vacuum pack with twice their weight of pickling liquor.

Place the cauliflower, turnip, tomatillo and radish into separate heatproof containers and pour over the hot pickling liquor. Allow to cool to room temperature and then cover and reserve, refrigerated.

For the egg
Boil the eggs for 9 minutes in salted water. Refresh, peel and press them through a ricer into a bowl. Add salt, mirin and lemon myrtle to taste. Reserve in an airtight container.

For the vegetable juice
Pass all the individual juices through a fine sieve (strainer), then combine them and add the mirin and salt – add more of these seasonings to taste if necessary. Blend in the xanthan gum at a ratio of 3g xanthan per 1 litre liquid, then pass the stock once more through a fine sieve (strainer) and keep refrigerated until service. At this point, add the finely sliced lovage leaves.

For the leaves
Pick everything down to the desired size (the leaves should be small, so everything is visually and texturally in balance), wash them in iced water and reserve, portioned, on absorbent paper.

To finish
Heat enough olive oil to submerge the calamari to a temperature of 55°C (131°F). Lay in the calamari to cook for 5 minutes, ensuring the oil temperature does not drop when the calamari goes in. Once cooked, transfer the calamari onto absorbent paper or cloth and curl it up so that the scored sides are facing out. Season with salt.

In the centre of each plate, build a little mound of the egg mix (no more than a teaspoonful per serve), then surround it with the pickles. Pour over enough vegetable juice to cover all the vegetables, then scatter over the leaves. Lay the calamari over the egg. Microplane the horseradish over the top and serve.

Clams in green tomato juice, chervil and lilly pilly

For 4 people

Fermented green tomato juice
(Makes enough to fill a 2-litre jar)
2 flowering heads of dill
8 horseradish leaves
1kg green tomatoes
purified water, at room
  temperature
salt
xanthan gum

Wakame oil
25g dried Tasmanian wakame
50g sea lettuce leaves
1.5 litres grapeseed oil

Barbecued clams
40-60 clams (based on size), such
  as South Australian vongole or
  preferably Goolwa pipis

Lilly pilly
12 small- to medium-sized
  lilly pilly fruit

Chervil
24 chervil leaves (or use bronze
  fennel if chervil is frost-affected)

For the fermented tomato juice

Sterilize your fermenting jar, then put the dill and horseradish into it. Tightly pack in the whole green tomatoes. Make enough brine to fill the jar and cover the tomatoes, using 2.5g salt per litre of water. Cover the tomatoes with the salt solution. Seal the jar well and leave at room temperature for at least 3 weeks.

Once the fermenting time has elapsed and when you are ready to prepare the tomatoes, prepare a barbecue.

Drain the green tomatoes, pat them dry and chargrill them so that they are blistered but not cooked. Transfer them directly to a juicer and extract their juice. Season to taste. Chill the juice immediately so that it does not oxidise. This recipe requires the juice to be thickened slightly so, once chilled, stir in 1g xanthan gum per litre of juice. Store it in a sealed container, refrigerated, until needed.

For the wakame oil

To hydrate the wakame, submerge it in 250ml water and leave it to stand for 1 hour. Drain the wakame and transfer it to a Thermomix along with the remaining ingredients. Process on a medium speed setting at 50°C (122°F) for 10 minutes.

Transfer the oil to a vacuum pack without straining it. Seal and leave to infuse at room temperature for 1 week. After the infusing time has elapsed, strain the solids from the oil. Store in an airtight container.

For the barbecued clams

Prepare a barbecue.

Put the clams into a perforated grill pan/basket and position this directly over a large mass of hot burning charcoals. It is important that the clams open quickly and are removed one by one as they open. Allow the coals to smoke the clams as they open but do not allow them to dry out.

Once the clams have all been removed from the heat, remove the meat from the shells, taking care not to tear it.

For the lilly pilly

Choose fruit that still has some green colour (they are more acidic, with herbal notes) rather than larger fully purple fruit that have developed more sweetness. Cut the fruit lengthways into halves and remove the seeds — take extra care to remove the fine but tough skin that comes away from the seed and occasionally sticks to the inside of the fruit. Allow 6 halves per serving.

For the chervil

Trim the leaves, leaving a little stem attached. Wash the leaves in iced water, dry them on absorbent paper and refrigerate in a sealed container until needed.

To finish

Place the clams in the middle of a shallow bowl and cover with enough green tomato juice so that they are completely dressed but still visible. Lay out the lilly pilly halves and cover each one with a chervil leaf. Dress liberally with wakame oil.

Egg yolk, potato and Jerusalem artichoke, sauce of Comté and vin jaune

For 4 people

Comté infusion
150g aged Comté cheese
300ml water
approximately 30ml vin jaune
salt, to taste

Egg yolk
olive oil
4 hens' eggs

Mushroom infusion
450g button mushrooms
400ml water

Potatoes
10 large Dutch Cream or
   Nicola potatoes

Pesto
125g hazelnuts
50ml sunflower oil
20ml hazelnut oil
20g browned butter
sea salt, to taste
about 225g Osaka or Green Elk
   mustard leaves

Jerusalem artichoke
2 Jerusalem artichokes
sunflower oil, for deep-frying
salt, to taste

Silverbeet
4 medium silverbeet or Perpetual
   Spinach leaves with stems
   attached
salt
olive oil

Wild cabbage flowers, per serve
10–15 wild cabbage flowers

For the Comté infusion
Remove the rind from the cheese and cut the cheese into small pieces. Combine the cheese and water in a Thermomix and process on a high speed at 50°C (122°F) for 10 minutes. Strain through a fine sieve (strainer) into a tall and narrow container and leave to settle overnight in the refrigerator. The cheese will settle into 3 sections – solids at the bottom, with water in the middle and then fat on the top. Remove both the water and the fat then discard the solids. Warm the fat and water whisking them together to achieve an homogeneous, fat-enriched cheese stock. Warm the solids, adding a splash of vin jaune to taste.

For the egg yolk
Prepare a water bath, bringing the water to 60°C (140°F).
   Pour olive oil into 4 small vials until they are about one-third full. Separate the yolks from the whites and put the yolks into the vials, ensuring they are completely submerged in the oil – top up with more oil if necessary. Place the lids on the vials and put them into the water bath. Keep warm until ready to serve.

For the mushroom infusion
Trim the base of the mushroom stems if they are dirty, then submerge the mushrooms in abundant water to remove any remaining impurities.
   Cut the mushrooms in half if necessary, with the aim of making them all a similar size. Combine them with the water in a saucepan. Cover with a cartouche and, over a medium heat, bring the infusion to a gentle simmer. You may need to weigh down the cartouche with a small tray or something similar so as to keep the mushrooms submerged until they become heavy with the water. Leave to simmer gently for 45 minutes, then strain and reduce the liquid by half.

For the potatoes
Peel the potatoes and cut them into smaller pieces. Using a pastry cutter or similar, trim the pieces into even-sized balls that measure approximately 2cm in diameter. Allow 5 balls per serve. Cook the potatoes in salted water (use 14g salt per litre of water) until just cooked. Strain and leave to cool to room temperature.

For the pesto
Preheat the oven to 140°C (285°F).
   Roast the hazelnuts for 20 minutes. Rub off the skins and combine the nuts with the oils and browned butter, adding salt to taste. Process the above in a food processor until smooth. Combine the mixture with an equal weight of chopped mustard leaves.

For the Jerusalem artichoke
Slice the artichokes finely on a mandoline. Deep-fry them at 140°C (285°F) until crisp but not too coloured. Drain them on absorbent paper and season to taste.

For the silverbeet
Blanch the leaves briefly in salted water, then dry them on absorbent paper or towel. Once dried, dress the leaves with olive oil, place them flat and evenly on the plancha to toast lightly. Season to taste.

To finish
Reduce the mushroom infusion with the potatoes until the potatoes are well glazed.
   Place a silverbeet leaf flat in the centre of each serving bowl and top with a spoonful of pesto. Arrange the glazed potatoes around the pesto, then place an egg yolk in the middle of the potatoes over the top of the pesto. Cover the egg and potatoes in each serving with 6g artichoke and pour around 15ml warm Comté infusion. Scatter over the wild cabbage flowers.

Eggplant in white miso, toasted grains, cured kelp

For 4 people

Toasted grains
400g sunflower oil
100g wild rice
50g quinoa
1 litre water
olive oil
salt, to taste
50g buckwheat

Aubergine (eggplant)
4 medium aubergines (eggplants)
Aubergine blanching liquor:
400ml dashi
15ml light soy sauce
5g caster sugar
4g salt
Aubergine marinade:
1 garlic clove
50g Valrhona Caraïbe dark
  chocolate
125g shiro (white) miso
60ml light soy sauce
30ml lemon juice
10ml Japanese pure sesame oil

Lemon confit
1 lemon
50g caster sugar
200ml rainwater

Kelp strips
reserved cooked kombu
  (see Simple Dashi on page 200)
100ml water
100g rendered pork fat
sea salt, to taste →

For the toasted grains

To prepare the puffed wild rice, warm the oil in a saucepan – it must reach 220°C (428°F) in order to puff the rice. Once the oil is at the desired temperature, stir in the rice and wait for it to puff. Once puffed, strain off the oil immediately and place the rice on absorbent paper. When the excess oil has been removed, place the puffed rice in a dehydrator and dehydrate at 55°C (131°F) for 4-6 hours.

Rinse the quinoa grains thoroughly under running water to remove the bitterness that is sometimes present.

Bring 500ml of the water to the boil and add the rinsed quinoa. Reduce the heat and allow the quinoa to simmer for 12 minutes. Strain the quinoa and chill immediately. When the quinoa is cool, dry it using absorbent paper.

Weigh the dried quinoa. Use 30ml olive oil per 100g quinoa to cook the quinoa without it becoming greasy. Heat the olive oil in a wide saucepan and toast the quinoa to a deep golden colour, ensuring that it is evenly toasted but not burnt. Spread the toasted quinoa on absorbent paper to remove any excess oil, season it, then store it in a sealed container until it is needed.

To cook the buckwheat, salt the remaining water, bring it to the boil and add the buckwheat. Boil rapidly for 8 minutes. Once the buckwheat is cooked, strain it and spread it on a tray to cool rapidly.

Warm a small amount of olive oil in a pan and add the cooked buckwheat, stirring continuously, until the buckwheat is toasted and has taken on a nutty flavour.

Transfer the toasted buckwheat to a dehydrator on non-stick dehydrator sheets and dehydrate at 55°C (131°F) for a minimum of 12 hours.

Once the grains are cooked and have been dehydrated, combine them (the ratio you have is 2 parts wild rice and 1 part quinoa to 1 part buckwheat). Check the seasoning and reserve in an airtight container until service.

For the aubergine (eggplant)

Peel the aubergines (eggplants) and cut them into even 10cm × 2.5cm × 2.5cm cylindrical pieces. Cook the aubergine cylinders in the blanching liquor for around 4–6 minutes.

To make the marinade, purée the garlic. Melt the chocolate in a heatproof bowl set over steam. Once the chocolate is liquid and the aubergine cylinders have cooked, take 100ml of the aubergine blanching liquor and combine it with the chocolate and the remaining marinade ingredients, stirring well to ensure that a homogenous paste is formed. Place enough marinade in a tray to cover the aubergine. Reserve the rest, vacuum sealed, in the refrigerator, to use for other dishes.

Remove the aubergine cylinders and place them, while still hot, into the marinade on the tray, ensuring that all pieces are completely covered. Reserve 100ml of the blanching liquor. Allow the aubergine cylinders to marinate for 6 hours.

For the lemon confit

Using a sharp paring knife, remove the rind from the lemon, taking care not to remove the bitter pith. Slice the peel into thin, even 3cm-long pieces.

Dissolve the sugar in the rainwater and place the lemon rind strips in the liquid. Over a very low heat, cook the lemon rind until the liquid thickens slightly and the rind has softened. Reserve in an airtight container.

For the kelp strips

Combine the reserved kombu with the water and pork fat and place the mixture in a vacuum pack. Braise the kombu at 80°C (176°F) for 12 hours. Once broken down and soft, cut the kombu into 10cm × 2mm strips. Reserve in a sealed container. →

Vegetables and leaves
4 × golden turnips
salt, to taste
4 × Purple Plum radish
4 × Breakfast radish
small sea lettuce leaves
assorted young brassica
   leaves such as nasturtium, Tokyo
   bekana, yukina savoy, purple
   choy,turnip and radish leaves
caster sugar

Serving broth
100ml reserved aubergine
blanching liquor (see above)
3g fresh (baker's) yeast

For the vegetables and leaves
Peel and blanch the baby turnips in salted boiling water. When just cooked, refresh them in iced water and cut them in half.
   Slice the radishes.
   Wash and dry the leaves, then separate them into 4 equal portions.
   Reserve the vegetables and leaves, refrigerated, until needed in service.

To serve
Preheat the oven to 140°C (285°F).
   Transfer the marinated aubergine cylinders to a baking tray and warm them in the oven. When they are heated through, burn them with a blowtorch – allow them to become quite black.
   Heat the reserved aubergine blanching liquor, then stir in the fresh (baker's) yeast.
   Place 1 aubergine cylinder in the centre of each shallow serving bowl. Cover it with a tablespoonful of the mixed toasted grains, allowing the grains to spill off the aubergine into the bowl.
   Caramelize the turnips, with cut sides facing down, in a little sugar, using just enough sugar to cover the base of the pan. Position 2 halves with each aubergine serving. Add some slices of radish, 2 pieces of lemon confit, the kelp strips and the leaves. Divide the hot aubergine blanching liquor into 4 equal portions, pour a portion over the aubergine in each bowl and serve.

Eggplant and saltgrass lamb washed with sweet onion juice, fragrant and acidic plants

For 4 people

Leek ash
2 medium-sized leeks, such as
   Jaune du Poitou or King Richard
olive oil
Note – these quantities yield more
   than is required, but this is a
   minimum amount to be practical

Honeycomb powder
125g sugar
63g glucose
30g spring-harvested pure honey
25ml water
7g bicarbonate of soda
(baking soda)

Dried sheep's yogurt
100g sheep's yogurt
3g leek ash (see above)
4g honeycomb powder
   (see above)
2g Davidson plum powder

Lovage oil
300g lovage leaf
50g parsley leaf
500ml olive oil
Note – these quantites yield more
oil than is required for this recipe

Aubergine (eggplant)
1 aubergine (eggplant)
tapioca starch
Sunflower oil, for frying
Aubergine blanching liquor:
400ml dashi
15ml light soy sauce
5g caster sugar
4g salt
Aubergine marinade:
1 garlic clove
50g Valrhona Caraïbe dark
   chocolate
125g shiro (white) miso
60ml light soy sauce
30ml lemon juice
10ml pure Japanese sesame oil

Lamb
60g saltgrass lamb from the rack
lemon-pressed olive oil
smoked olive oil
lemon myrtle powder
sansho powder
oyster powder

Onion juice
2kg large brown onions
olive oil
egg white
xanthan gum
salt
Japanese brown rice vinegar →

For the leek ash
Follow the instructions on page 120 to make the leek ash.

For the honeycomb powder
Follow the instructions on page 232 for making honeycomb powder only, instead of bashing the honeycomb to a powder with a rolling pin, process it to a fine powder in a food processor.

For the dried sheep's yogurt
Place the sheep's yogurt into ricotta baskets or a sieve (strainer) lined with absorbent cloth and leave to hang over a bowl for around 48–72 hours. Once the whey has been removed the resulting curd will be drier and have an increased intensity of flavour.
   Combine the dried yogurt with the remaining ingredients.

For the lovage oil
Follow the instructions on page 194 to make the lovage oil.

For the aubergine (eggplant)
Follow the instructions on page 174 to prepare the aubergine (eggplant) but cut the aubergine to 8cm × 2.5cm × 2.5cm cylindrical pieces.

For the lamb
Follow the instructions on page 194 to slice and store the lamb.

For the onion juice
Preheat the oven to 70°C (158°F). Prepare a barbecue.
   Slice the onions in half through the skins and across the cores. Rub the flesh of the onions with a small amount of oil. Place the onions, flesh-side down, on a plancha and cook until blackened. Once black, transfer the onions to a barbecue. Set them slightly above the heat and allow the water inside the onions to boil.
   When the water begins to bubble out of the onions, transfer them to a stainless steel bowl and cover with clingfilm (plastic wrap). Leave them to steam in the bowl.
   Remove the cooled onions from the bowl and, with the back of a paring knife, remove all traces of carbon. This step is important as any blackness will result in an overly bitter stock. Remove the skins and put the cleaned onions in a stainless steel bowl, wrap the bowl tightly with clingfilm and transfer to the oven. Bake for 12 hours, leaving the onions to steam slowly and their sugars to caramelise.
   Once the baking time has elapsed, remove the onions from the oven and push them several times through a juicer, extracting as much juice as possible, then pass the juice through a fine chinois.
   Mix the egg white with the juice at a ratio of 100g white to 1 litre juice. Put the mixture into a vacuum pack sealed without vacuum.
   Set a steam oven to 100°C (212°F). Transfer the vacuum pack to the steam oven and cook for around 2 hours. You can place the sealed bag into a pan of boiling water and boil it hard for the same period of time – just be careful the pan does not boil dry. The protein in the egg white will set during this period and clarify the liquid. Once the albumen is set and patches of clear liquid appear, remove the liquid from the bag and strain it through a fine sieve (strainer). Thicken the juice with xanthan gum at a ratio of 4g xanthan gum per litre liquid. Season with salt. Add vinegar to taste. →

Pickled garlic
30g caster sugar
50ml white wine vinegar
12ml lemon juice
10ml lime juice
125ml water
4 large cloves of garlic

Fragrant and acidic plants,
per serve
a good mixture of sansho, bone
fruit clusters, salty ice plant buds
and leaves, different basils, sorrels,
Vietnamese mint, spearmint,
Morrocan mint, society garlic
flowers and chive flowers

For the pickled garlic

Dissolve the sugar in the vinegar and citrus juices and combine with the water. Peel the garlic, place the cloves into a small vacuum bag and cover with the pickling liquor.

Set a water bath to 85°C (185°F) and cook the garlic for 20 minutes. Once this time has passed, remove the bag from the heat and chill immediately.

When cool, remove the garlic from the pickle and slice it finely into even 'rounds' on a mandoline. Return the garlic slices to the pickling liquor and leave in a sealed container until needed.

To finish

Preheat the oven to 140°C (284°F).

Transfer the marinated aubergine cylinders to a baking tray and warm them in the oven. When they are hot through, burn them with a blowtorch — they can become quite black. Dust the pieces in tapioca starch and deep-fry for 2 minutes at 180°C (356°F) until the starch is cooked.

Heat the onion juice.

Dress the lamb slices with the lemon and smoked oils, ensuring the meat is coated right up to the edges. Season well with the lemon myrtle, sansho and oyster powders and salt.

Place a little dried yogurt mix on each plate, then the fried aubergine, and drape the lamb over the top. Place the pickled garlic on the lamb and spoon over a little warm onion juice, then drizzle lovage oil over the onion juice so that it beads rather than emulsifies. Scatter with the leaves and flowers then serve.

Southern rock lobster and burnt potatoes

Spring and early summer isn't all just green and chlorophyll. At this time of year I'm also thinking about the changes in the ocean, the local crays coming back into season, the fish roe, particularly that found in the deep-water flathead caught south west of here off the Great Ocean Road coast, and the flowering pastures in these parts that are grazed by Jersey and Friesian cattle.

And I think about the potatoes that are prolific in the Otways on a commercial level, but which have to be one of the greatest vegetables to cook and eat when just harvested from your own garden, their skins paper-thin and tasting of earth, and their flesh sweet, firm and waxy. With an older potato that's been harvested with a thicker skin and stored for a while, and which has a higher starch content, I prefer to drown it in olive oil or eat it crisp-roasted, but when potatoes are young or new and harvested just as the plants start to flower and are still small enough to fit a dozen or so in your hand, there seems to be nothing better than coating them with butter, cultured cream or milk that's been caramelized.

The main agriculture in the Otway hinterland and heading west for a couple of hundred kilometres is dairy. This rich, fertile belt is located south of the main highway and stretches all the way from here to Warrnambool, getting all the regular rain that this part of Australia is known for, but is inland just far enough to escape the salt mists off the sea. I've found a real reconnection to dairy since living and working here and, as a result, milk in different guises appears in far more dishes at Brae than I can remember at any other restaurant I've worked at. As a kid I drank a lot of milk – not that I remember it being particularly good, it was super-homogenised to be tasteless. And I remember all the hysteria in the 1980s onwards about low-fat and no-fat milk products and higher rates of lactose intolerance. Being in Western Victoria for ten years now, I've been able to see dairy farms and meet dairy farmers and have access to milk and cream of a quality I don't remember seeing before in the food chain in Australia – not in my lifetime, anyway.

I buy milk and cream from Simon Schulz, who runs the same property his grandfather farmed. An organic, biodynamic operation since 1971, with just under 1,000 acres and based in Timboon, this farm produces a product I consider to be peerless in these parts. Un-homogenised but pasteurized (unfortunately, a legal requirement in Australia) to the minimum time and temperature, the milk, cream and yogurt always arrives with a lashing of fat on top and, thankfully, still tasting of what it is and of the time of year. It's interesting to spend time at the Schulz farm. In spring, after driving through a fairly typical mainstream commercial agricultural area just north of them, with 'perfect' mono-pasture paddocks, I arrive to see mixed grasses in flower, bees and life all around. I am reminded that this is what a healthy piece of land should look like – even while it's being worked or farmed, and that so-called weeds (read: pasture diversity) are totally OK, and that the animals probably rely on this for health. And I am reminded that good farming practice is not about short grass under fence lines – it's about conscientious management of land, of animal and human health, and it's also about environmental diversity.

In this recipe we simmer just-harvested waxy potatoes, like Pink Fir or young Kipflers, rub off their skins but not fastidiously, dry them slightly to reduce some of the water content and then marinate them in cream infused with horseradish. Once we're that happy the flavour of the cream has penetrated the potatoes, we burn them with a blowtorch, caramelizing the milk sugars and giving the potatoes a charred note. Whipped fish roe is laid on the plate amongst the potatoes, followed by the lobster. It is all enriched with shavings of cured egg yolk. At the end a milk skin is laid over the top, hiding all the other ingredients, and grassy spring herbs – tarragon, different fennels and sunflower or Jerusalem artichoke petals – are placed over the skin to hopefully accentuate that milk comes from grass, and to give a snapshot of the flavour of spring in the Otways and Western Victoria.

Southern rock lobster and burnt potatoes, flathead roe, milk and mustard

For 4 people

Potato marinade
150g soured cream
15g Microplaned horseradish
5ml lemon juice

Potatoes
8 small Kipfler or Bintje potatoes,
   weiging approximately 30g each
salt

Flathead roe cream
200g flathead roe
salt
1 litre water
125g white onions, finely sliced
   and cooked in whey until
   completely soft
300ml reduced whey
25ml cider vinegar
4g gellan gum
salt, to taste

Southern rock lobster
1 live southern rock lobster
   (crayfish), weighing 1kg
This quantity yields more meat
than required for this recipe but
is a minimum size to work with

Milk skins
1 litre whole (full-fat) milk
50ml cream mixed with 25ml
   whole (full-fat) milk →

For the potato marinade
Mix the ingredients together.

For the potatoes
Peel the potatoes, place them in a pan of salted water (use 14g salt per 1 litre water) and simmer gently until just cooked – it is important that a skewer passes through with no resistance.

Remove the potatoes and allow to cool to room temperature, then dehydrate them at 55°C (131°F) for around 4 hours.

Once semi-dried, rub the potatoes liberally with the marinade and vacuum seal them on maximum pressure. Leave them to marinate for around 12 hours.

At the time of serving, char the potatoes with a blowtorch until the marinade is lightly scorched and the potatoes have a burnt-milk aroma.

For the flathead roe cream
Scrape the roe into a stainless steel bowl. Prepare the brine using a ratio of 1 part salt to 10 parts water. Cover the roe with cold brine, stirring it to separate all the eggs. Leave to brine for 1 hour, then strain off.

Heat the water in a saucepan to 70°C (158°F) and stir in 150g of the brined roe, stirring continuously. Ensure the temperature remains at 70°C (158°F) and cook for 15 minutes. Strain the cooked roe through a fine conical strainer and chill rapidly.

Combine the pasteurized roe with the other ingredients, except the seasoning, in a Thermomix and process at 95°C (203°F) for 5 minutes. Pour the hot mixture onto a small tray and cool rapidly, leaving to cool and set in the refrigerator for at least 3 hours.

Once completely cold and set firm, return the mix to the Thermomix and process on a medium to high speed setting until a smooth, homogenous cream is achieved. Check the seasoning before reserving the roe cream.

For the southern rock lobster
Place the lobster in an ice slurry to put it to sleep. Once it is unconscious, take a large knife and cut through the head between the eyes, ensuring that it is killed humanely and quickly. Remove the tail from the body and wrap both the tail and head in absorbent paper. Place the head and the tail into separate vacuum packs, taking care not to puncture the bags, and seal with maximum pressure.

Cook the southern rock lobster in a water bath set at 61°C (142°F). At this temperature, the tail of a 1kg lobster will take 23½ minutes to cook, while the head and body will need 27 minutes (for every 100g over 1kg add 2½ minutes to the cooking time).

Once cooked, remove the bags from the water and refresh them in a blast chiller or ice slurry, leaving the crayfish to cool for at least 45 minutes. Ensure that the centre of each piece is completely cold.

Use scissors to cut open the shell of the tail, then remove the meat in 1 piece. With the head and legs, for maximum yield, break them down completely and remove all the meat. Chop the tail meat and add it to the leg and head meat. Divide the meat into 4 × 25g portions. Reserve, refrigerated until needed.

For the milk skins
Preheat the oven (low fan) to 110°C (230°F).

Put the milk into a wide-based rectangular pan (hotel pan) and leave it in the oven for 1½ hours. The milk will form a skin. Remove the tray from the oven, taking care not to break the skin, and cover it with a sheet of greaseproof (wax) paper that has been brushed with the milk-and-cream mixture. Once the skin is stuck to the paper, lift the paper carefully to remove the milk skin from the surface of the milk. Place another sheet of paper on top and leave the skin to cool and harden. Once cold, cut the sheet into 12cm × 12cm squares. →

Mustard seeds
20g yellow mustard seeds
   reduced whey

Radishes
4 Pink Beauty or Watermelon
   radishes
salt, for brining
100ml dry cider, heated until
   the alcohol is cooked off

Seasonings
salt
crustacean powder
bottarga
cured egg yolk
horseradish

Leaves, herbs and flowers,
per serve
chopped chives
3 fine rocket (arugula) leaves
4 bronze fennel fronds
4 Florence fennel fronds
4 dill fronds
3 tarragon leaves
6–8 sunflower petals

To serve
cider vinegar, to taste
olive oil

For the mustard seeds

Blanch the seeds from cold several times to help remove some of their bitterness. Cover them with water and simmer gently for 3 hours until soft. Strain off the water and reserve the mustard seeds in reduced whey. They can be stored in the fridge for up to 3 days.

For the radishes

Compress the radishes whole in a brine made using 1 part salt to 20 parts water. Leave to sit for 1 hour. Remove them and cut them into very fine, almost transparent, rounds, then marinate them in the cider just prior to serving.

To serve

Warm the lobster meat and season it with salt and crustacean powder.

Place a small spoonful of the flathead roe cream on each serving plate, then the warmed potatoes. Place a portion of the southern rock lobster on the roe and between the potatoes and scatter some mustard seeds, radish rounds, shaved bottarga and shaved egg yolk over the top. Lay a milk skin over the other ingredients so that everything is hidden, then shave a little horseradish over the skin. Scatter with some chives, then the other herbs, leaves and flowers and dress with both cider vinegar and olive oil.

Southern rock lobster cooked with carrot and sea butter

For 4 people

Southern rock lobster (crayfish)
1 live southern rock lobster
  (crayfish), weighing around
  1.2–1.5kg

Sea butter
200g salted butter, at room
  temperature
4g sea lettuce powder
(see page 82)

Crustacean salt
75g masa harina
50ml water
400g roasted and dehydrated
  prawn heads
2.5g sea lettuce powder

Carrot juice and pieces
200g large Danvers carrots
  or similar
xanthan gum
salt, to taste
2 medium Yellow Lobbericher
  carrots or similar
butter, for cooking

Onions
2 small white pickling-size onions

Olives
8 Manzanilla olives

Leaves
16 golden purslane leaves
  with stems
24 olive plant leaves

For the southern rock lobster

Place the lobster in an ice slurry to put it to sleep. Once it is unconscious, take a large knife and cut through the head between the eyes, ensuring that it is killed humanely and quickly. Remove the tail from the body and wrap both the tail and head in absorbent paper. Place the head and the tail into separate vacuum packs, taking care not to puncture the bags, and seal with maximum pressure.

Cook the southern rock lobster in a water bath set at 61°C (142°F). At this temperature, the tail of a 1kg lobster will take 23½ minutes to cook, while the head and body will need 27 minutes (for every 100g over 1kg add 2½ minutes to the cooking time).

Once cooked, remove the bags from the water and refresh them in a blast chiller or ice slurry, leaving the crayfish to cool for at least 45 minutes. Ensure that the centre of each piece is completely cold.

Use scissors to cut open the shell of the tail, then remove the meat in 1 piece. With the head and legs, for maximum yield, break them down completely and remove all the meat. Chop the tail meat and add it to the leg and head meat. Divide the meat into 4 × 25g portions. Reserve, refrigerated until needed.

For the sea butter

Combine the butter with the sea lettuce powder in a food processor. Store refrigerated in a sealed container.

For the crustacean salt

Preheat the oven to 170°C (338°F).

Mix the masa harina with the water (you are working with a ratio of 1 part water to 1.25 parts masa harina) to make a dough. Roll this thinly between sheets of parchment, then bake for around 12 minutes until completely dry.

Process the baked masa powder with the remaining ingredients in a food processor. Pass the resulting powder through a fine sieve (strainer), sifting out any large pieces. Reserve in an airtight container.

For the carrot juice and pieces

Juice the carrots, then strain out any fibre so the juice is completely smooth. Combine the juice with xanthan gum at a ration of 3g xanthan gum to 1 litre juice and season to taste. Reserve, refrigerated.

Prepare the carrot rounds. Place the washed but unpeeled whole Yellow Lobbericher carrots in a saucepan with some butter and a little water and set the pan over a low heat. Allow the butter to start to foam, then control the heat so that the water/butter emulsion does not reduce too quickly or start to brown. Baste the carrots until they are just cooked, then remove the pan from the heat. While the carrots are still warm, rub off the skins. Slice the carrots into even rounds, allowing around 6 pieces per portion.

For the onions

Preheat the oven to 140°C (284°F).

Wrap the onions in foil and bake them until soft. Peel them and separate the layers, removing the thin fibre on the inside of each layer. Allow 3–4 pieces per portion, depending on size.

For the olives

Pit the olives and dice them into small pieces.

For the leaves

Wash the leaves in iced water, dry them on absorbent paper and refrigerate in a sealed container until needed.

To serve

Place a little of the sea butter to warm in a saucepan over a medium heat, add the olives, then the lobster and carrots, stirring gently so that everything is well coated in the sea butter. Distribute the southern rock lobster and carrots evenly between 4 bowls and sprinkle a little of the crustacean salt over each. Add some warmed onion pieces and spoon over some carrot juice, finishing with the leaves.

Jumbuck

A few years ago, I was talking with one of my long-time suppliers, Anthony from Greenvale Farm, about how mainstream consumer Australian meat-eating habits (unfortunately, for the most part, dictated and driven by a couple of our big supermarkets) had led us down a path to meat that, for my taste, is generally too young, flavourless and without personality. Nearly all meat that's sold in supermarkets and even in many butcher's shops falls into this category, with the minor exception being some of the beef (mainly due to the fact that it's the most consumed meat in Australia), which carries a bit more consumer pressure and is also currently receiving its highest price ever per kilo. As a result, even at the lower end there are competing specialist beef brands that, at least through their marketing, focus a bit more on flavour.

Where I find we really miss out is with lamb. It seems that for too long, many producers have just grown stock – something to hit a minimum age and weight and then get to market with no real interest in where it ends up, who eats it and, ultimately, how it tastes. I'm not sure if there's a correlation but, certainly, there's been a decrease in the amount of wool produced in western Victoria over the last thirty years, and a simultaneous increase in the number of lambs being eaten, and I would suspect that the same people who once grew wool now grow plenty of fat lambs, which is obviously a different game in regards to genetics and feed and maybe, on some small scale, this contributes to the marketplace being full of younger, average-tasting product. Over time, too, the meat has become leaner. Lamb is now trimmed much more for presentation. And I guess with a faster-paced lifestyle, consumers want to cook simply and quickly, want softer and easier-to-prepare cuts of meat, with less waste and mess (i.e. less time preparing and no time for fat rendering). Consumers now have smaller families and fewer people to feed, and with marketing and advertising from all sides of food production trying to convince us that 'quick-and-easy' is the best type of food, the demand for younger, smaller lambs has grown.

At this stage, Anthony was not a fully-fledged pig farmer and was still running some fat lambs. In the course of a few conversations we agreed the lamb we both preferred to eat for flavour which, from a chef's perspective, is generally why you eat, was mutton or hogget. The average lamb typically eaten in Australia is from a carcass weighing around 18–20kg and has been slaughtered at around twelve months old. We were interested in animals that were at least twice that age, maybe more, and certainly much bigger in size. Anthony grew a few out to the age of two or two-and-a-half years and gave me some to try, shoulders and legs mainly. They were some of the most delicious roasts I remember having at home in recent years, with an aroma that reminded me of the roasts my mum cooked when I was a child, which makes me think that all those roast lambs were probably mutton – there are a lot of people of my mum's generation who do say they prefer the flavour of mutton.

After trying a few different cuts of Anthony's mutton I had an idea that we should dry-age it and see how it developed. Most lamb would be hung for seven days maximum, but a longer hanging time works for older beef. All of Anthony's mutton has grazed on grass, they're large beast and have great protective fat caps, so it seemed logical to give it a try. At the same time, Anthony mentioned that he had some really old animals that, over time, had gotten away from the rest of the flock and were basically free ranging in other parts of his property.

I think he probably said it at first as a joke, to see what I would say – they were at least four years old, potentially five, and to me this sounded great. Always looking to diversify and for a niche market, he suggested we give a couple of them a go. If they were any good, he decided, he would market and sell them as Jumbuck, a word used by Banjo Paterson in the ballad *Waltzing Matilda*. The term was thought to be derived from an indigenous language used by early settlers to describe what you'd imagine would have been older sheep.

It's common that at one year, a sheep gets an incisor tooth and becomes mutton and, at two, it gets a second and becomes hogget. After that, there's not really any classification or name for these beasts, so Anthony was probably right to name them. The first couple came in dressed at around 55kg, from memory, and had five incisors, basically a full set of teeth. Dry-aged for thirty-five days, the meat was rich and ever so slightly oily, heavily marbled like good beef and with a depth of flavour that went on and on. It was the best lamb, hogget or jumbuck I've ever eaten. The fillet was surprisingly soft and in no way chewy or tough. It was actually soft enough that – to do this great example of an idea, farming, product and process any justice – I thought I should serve it raw to preserve its qualities.

It's an unfamiliar combination to serve old lamb with raw white fish, but the garnish suits both proteins without any issues and the textures of these two are almost identical, so the textural game has this great confusing quality to it as you chew on both the flathead and the jumbuck, waiting for their flavours to come through.

Cooking the jumbuck is also a delicious process. The intramuscular fat slowly renders to baste the meat. Given its period of dry-aging, it can tend to dry out if cooked over charcoal too slowly, but keeping an eye on it, and only taking it to medium-rare, then dressing it with a fat such as the bonito mayonnaise that follows takes care of that.

Dry-aged jumbuck and flathead sashimi, broccoli and salted dandelion

For 4 people

Salted dandelion
250ml water
40g salt
125g wild dandelion buds
Note – these quantites yield
enough for around 30 portions,
but are the minimum quantities
to be working with

Horseradish cream
60g crème fraîche
4g grated horseradish
3ml lemon juice
10g finely chopped salted capers,
  pre-rinsed and soaked to remove
  excess salt
4g finely chopped fennel fronds
4g finely chopped parsley
2g finely chopped French tarragon
Note – these quantites yield
enough for around 8 portions but
it is difficult to make a smaller
amount

Jumbuck
60g 4–5 week dry-aged
  Greenvale Farm Jumbuck fillet or
  boneless rack (minimum 4 year
  old/4-tooth), or use lamb fillet
40ml lemon-pressed olive oil
10ml smoked olive oil
1g ground sansho pepper
salt, to taste

Flathead
1 fillet from a 1kg line-caught
  flathead, skin off and pin-boned
  (note that you can usually get
  around 6 portions from 1 fillet)
salt, to taste

Broccoli
16 purple sprouting broccoli
  florets with 3–4cm stems
olive oil

Broccoli juice
500g broccoli stems
1g xanthan gum
salt, to taste

Oyster powder
4 Pacific oysters

Leaves and flowers
32 young assorted broccoli leaves
32 broccoli flowers or other
  brassica flowers
32 wild garlic flowers or three-
  cornered leek flowers

For the salted dandelion
Bring the water and salt to a boil, then pour over the dandelion buds. Discard any buds that open. Seal the buds in the brine in a vacuum pack for a minimum of 4 days and a maximum of 1 month.

For the horseradish cream
Combine the crème fraîche and horseradish and leave to infuse for a minimum of 12 hours. Pass the cream through a fine mesh sieve (strainer) to remove any horseradish particles, then add the remaining ingredients and adjust the seasoning as necessary. (Note that it is important to ensure that the capers are fully rinsed of salt. If not, this dish can end up being over-seasoned.)

For the jumbuck
Slice the jumbuck into 4 even rounds across the fillet. Place each slice between 2 × 10cm squares of greaseproof (wax) paper. Using the flat side of a meat mallet or the back of a small saucepan, hammer the jumbuck down to very thin, round pieces. Reserve the jumbuck, refrigerated, between the greaseproof paper sheets, until needed, ensuring that the edges do not dry out.

For the flathead
Cut the flathead across the fillet into even 5g pieces, allowing 3 pieces per portion. Reserve the portions, covered and refrigerated, until needed.

For the broccoli
When selecting and preparing the broccoli, ensure all the broccoli florets are formed but not too open and that all the stems are finished with a clean cut. Wash the broccoli of any grit and reserve it, portioned, in dariole moulds or similar until service.

For the broccoli juice
Juice the broccoli and return the pulp several times through the juicer to maximize yield.
Strain the juice through a fine mesh sieve (strainer) and combine 250ml of the juice with 1g xanthan gum in a Thermomix, working it slowly for around 10 minutes until the xanthan is fully hydrated. Season, taste and strain the juice to remove any leftover particles of xanthan gum. Reserve the juice in a container, covered and chilled, until needed.

For the oyster powder
Shuck the oysters and rinse them in their own juice, removing any fragments of shell. Place them in a dehydrator and dehydrate at 55°C (131°F) for a minimum of 48 hours.
Once fully dry, process the oysters on a high speed setting in a food processor until they become a fine power. Pass the powder through a fine sieve (strainer) to remove larger pieces. Reserve the powder in an airtight container.

For the leaves and flowers
Wash the leaves, pat them dry on absorbent paper and portion them, using 8 leaves of different sizes per portion. Cut the flowers from the broccoli and also the wild garlic, leaving at least 1cm of stem attached to each one. Portion them, allowing 8 flowers of each type per portion. These can be portioned together. Reserve both the flowers and leaves, covered and refrigerated, until needed.

To serve
Remove the top layer of greaseproof paper from the jumbuck and dress it with first lemon oil, then a little smoked oil, sansho and salt.
Season the flathead with salt only.
Blanch the broccoli in salted boiling water for around 10 seconds, dry it off, then dress it with olive oil.
In the centre of each flat, round serving plate, place 1 teaspoon of horseradish cream and spread it into an 8–10cm round. Drizzle a little broccoli juice over the top and place 3 pieces of flathead on top. Drape the jumbuck over the flathead and cover it with 3–5 salted dandelion buds, the broccoli, the broccoli leaves, a dusting of oyster powder and, finally, the flowers.

Dry-aged jumbuck, beans and barbecued lettuce

For 4 people

Jumbuck
1 boneless rack of dry-aged
jumbuck or lamb

Bonito mayonnaise
50g bonito or tuna preserved
  in olive oil
3 egg yolks
5g Dijon mustard
25ml Chardonnay vinegar
filtered water
375ml olive oil
salt, to taste
mixture of equal parts dill,
  tarragon and parsley leaves,
  finely chopped, to taste
Note – these quantities yield a
little more than is needed for this
recipe, but this is the minimum
amount that can be processed

Barbecued lettuce
salt
1 cos lettuce heart, quartered
smoked olive oil

Whole lemon purée
2 large lemons (approximately
350g total weight)
150ml soy milk
4.5g gellan gum
salt, to taste

Broad bean purée
375g blanched double-shelled
  broad (fava) beans
65g roasted hazelnut purée
  (roasted, peeled and processed
  hazelnuts) or hazelnut paste
135g sheep's curd (sheep's yogurt
  that has been hung to remove
  water content – see page 120)
25ml lemon juice
salt, to taste

Beans
100g double-shelled baby broad
  (fava) beans or a mixture of
  yellow, Romano and baby broad
  beans (depending on season)
olive oil
salt

Seasonings
oyster powder (see page 190)
anchovy water

For the jumbuck
Prepare a barbecue.
  Seal the fillet on a plancha, and then roast it to medium-rare on the barbecue – ensure you stop cooking when the internal temperature reaches 52°C (125°F).

For the bonito mayonnaise
Combine the drained bonito, yolks, mustard, vinegar and a splash of filtered cold water and process in a food processor on a high speed setting until a tight emulsion is formed. Slowly stream in the oil to create a mayonnaise. Season to taste and add water to achieve the desired taste and texture. Add the herbs to taste – this mayonnaise should taste quite herby.

For the barbecued lettuce
Prepare a barbecue.
  Prepare the brine using a ratio of 1 part salt to 20 parts water. Submerge the lettuce quarters (or halves, depending on the size of the lettuce heart) and leave for at least 1 hour. Remove the lettuce quarters, pat them dry and seal the cut sides on the plancha. Brush them with smoked oil and transfer to the chargrill, ensuring that they remain al dente and take on plenty of the barbecue aromas.

For the whole lemon purée
Follow the instructions on page 142 to prepare the whole lemon purée.

For the broad bean purée
Combine all the ingredients, except the salt, in a food processor and process to a thick purée. It is important that the broad (fava) beans are sufficiently cooked before processing or else they can render the purée excessively starchy. Season as needed.

For the beans
Prepare and blanch the beans as required, then trim them to even pieces. Warm them in olive oil, then season to taste.

To serve
Warm the lettuce quarters over the barbecue, portion them into 4 equal pieces and place each of these pieces in the centre of each plate. On either side of the lettuce, place a little of both purées, and then spoon over the warmed beans.
  Slice the jumbuck into ribbons length-ways on a meat slicer and dress the pieces liberally with the bonito mayonnaise. Drape 3–4 slices of jumbuck over the lettuce on each plate. Sprinkle over the oyster powder, add a light drizzling of anchovy water and serve.

Artichoke and saltgrass lamb washed with mussel juice and citrus

For 4 people

Lovage oil
300g lovage leaves
50g parsley leaves
500ml olive oil
Note – these quantities yield more
oil than is required for this recipe

Artichokes
4 small globe artichokes
ascorbic acid
tapioca starch
sunflower oil, for deep-frying

Artichoke purée
260g globe artichoke halves
4g gellan gum
1 litre water
75ml olive oil
salt, to taste

Lamb
60g saltgrass lamb from the rack
lemon-pressed olive oil
smoked olive oil
oyster powder (see page 190)
sansho powder
lemon myrtle leaf powder
salt, to taste

Mussel juice
450g mussels
325ml water
15g lemongrass
17g ginger
1 kaffir lime leaf

Leaves per serving
5 sansho leaves
2 bone fruit clusters
3 salty ice plant buds and leaves
small amount of lovage leaf,
finely sliced

For the lovage oil
Blanch the lovage and parsley leaves quickly in boiling water, then refresh them in an ice slurry. Once chilled, squeeze out the excess water, combine the leaves with the olive oil in a Thermomix and process at 50°C (122°F) using a high speed setting for 5 minutes. Line a fine sieve (strainer) with muslin, then suspend it over a container. Add the processed herbs and oil, then fold the top of the cloth over itself. Place a weight of some description, such as a pan, a heavy stone or a sealed jug of water, to add weight and press the herbs so as to extract the maximum amount of oil. Leave to stand until all the oil has filtered through.

Reserve the green oil in a sealed container for a maximum of 3–4 days.

For the artichokes
Remove the outer leaves of the artichokes, trim the stems and place the hearts into an acidulated solution, made using 1g ascorbic acid to 1 litre of water, to avoid oxidisation.

Place the artichokes and a little of the ascorbic liquor into a vacuum pack and seal tightly. Steam for 15–18 minutes or until cooked. Plunge into an ice bath or chill rapidly in a blast chiller. Keep sealed and refrigerated until needed.

For the artichoke purée
Prepare the artichokes as described above, but cook them for around 40 minutes. Chill as described above. Combine the gellan gum with the water. Remove the artichokes from the vacuum pack, combine them with the gellan gum solution and process to a purée. Once broken down a little, start streaming in the olive oil, as much as you would if making a mayonnaise. Transfer the emulsion to a saucepan and heat it to 85°C (185°F) to activate the gellan.

Spread the purée across a tray. Refrigerate until cooled and hardened. After a minimum of 3 hours, return the hardened mix to a food processor and process on a high speed setting until a thick, fatty purée is achieved. Season to taste with salt. Keep chilled until ready to use.

For the lamb
Slice the lamb into 4 even rounds across the fillet and place between 2 × 10cm squares of greaseproof (wax) paper. Using the flat side of a meat mallet or the back of a small saucepan, hammer the lamb down to very thin round pieces. Reserve the lamb, refrigerated, between the sheets of greaseproof paper until needed, ensuring the edges do not dry out.

For the mussel juice
Scrub the mussels with steel wool, ensuring that all barnacles and grit are completely removed, and rinse the mussels in fresh water. Place them in a saucepan with the water. Place a lid on the pan and, over a low heat, bring the liquid to a very gentle simmer. Allow the stock to simmer for around 40 minutes and for the juices from the mussels to combine and cook with the water.

Strain the resulting liquid through a fine sieve (strainer) and chill it rapidly.

To finish the mussel juice, roughly chop the other ingredients and then bring 500ml of the mussel juice to the boil. Pour the stock over the aromatics and leave to stand, sealed, for around 45 minutes. When infused sufficiently, strain off the aromatics. Chill the mussel juice until needed.

To finish
Dust the artichokes with tapioca starch and deep-fry them at 180°C (356°F) for around 1 minute, crisping the starch but not allowing it to colour.

Remove the lamb slices from the paper and dress with the lemon and smoked oils, ensuring the meat is coated right to the edges. Season well with the oyster, sansho and lemon myrtle powders and salt.

Place a spoonful (roughly 30g) artichoke purée on each serving plate. Divide the fried artichoke into 4 portions and add a portion to each serving plate, placing it over the purée, then drape the lamb over. Spoon over a little heated mussel juice split with lovage oil, then scatter over the leaves.

Grass-fed Wagyu and salted radish, rock samphire and Otway shiitake

For 4 people

Pickled rock samphire
50ml Chardonnay vinegar
30ml lemon juice
50ml lime juice
125ml water
32g caster sugar
100g rock samphire

Wagyu short rib
rack of 4 short ribs from
   pasture-raised Wagyu beef

Veal stock
10kg veal knuckle bones
olive or sunflower oil
8kg stewing beef
1.6kg large carrots
3.7kg brown onions
650g large, ripe tomatoes
25 litres water
1 pork trotter
½ calf's foot, split
Note – these quantities yield
more stock than is required for
this recipe but this is
a minimum amount to make

Glaze
100g shallots
20g ginger
25ml Japanese sesame oil
2g red Szechuan pepper
50ml maple syrup
100ml sake
400g eel meat and bones
2.5 litres veal stock (see above)
salt, to taste

Salted radish
5g salt
100ml water
10 radishes (can be of different
   varieties, such as Cherry Belle
   and French Breakfast)

Shiitake
8 large shiitake mushrooms
olive oil
salt, to taste

Mushroom and sansho powder
mushroom trimmings
   (see method)
sansho powder or lemon myrtle
leaf powder →

For the pickled rock samphire
Warm the liquids and dissolve the sugar in them. Pour the mixture over the samphire. Leave in a sealed container for at least 1 week before using.

For the Wagyu
Wrap the piece of beef in kitchen (aluminum) foil so that the bones do not puncture the vacuum pack and then seal in a vacuum pack on maximum pressure. Place the short rib into a water bath and cook for 24 hours at 72°C (162°F).

After this time, when the meat is soft, remove the short rib and, while hot, slide the bones out. Leave the meat to cool and firm up.

Cut the meat into rectangular portions of around 70g. Place the portions in a vacuum pack once more so that they can be warmed for service.

For the veal stock
Preheat the oven to 200°C (390°F).

Rub the veal bones with oil and roast them to a deep golden, turning them as necessary and draining off excessive amounts of fat.

Cut the beef into large pieces, coat it with oil and roast to a deep brown.

Peel the carrots and onions. Roast the carrots whole. Halve the onions and roast them until dark.

Halve the tomatoes and roast them until dark in colour.

Place all roasted ingredients into a large stockpot with the remaining ingredients and bring to a gentle simmer. Skim any fat and impurities from the surface and simmer for 12 hours. Ensure the stock never boils hard and skim it regularly during the cooking time.

Once the stock has cooked for the prescribed time, pass it first through a coarse sieve (strainer), then a fine one, then return it to the stove to reduce. Continue to skim any impurities from the surface and reduce the liquid to 5 litres.

Pass the stock once again through a fine strainer and cool rapidly. Reserve until needed.

For the glaze
Slice the shallots and ginger.

Warm the sesame oil in a wide saucepan and slowly sweat the shallots and ginger without colouring. Add the Szechuan pepper, then the maple syrup and allow to lightly caramelize.

Deglaze with the sake. Add the eel, then the veal stock. Bring the stock to a gentle simmer and cook out slowly, skimming impurities that surface. Reduce the stock as it cooks to 750ml. Pass it through a fine sieve (strainer), season to taste and chill rapidly.

For the salted radish
Dissolve the salt in the water and combine with the whole radishes in a vacuum pack. Compress on maximum pressure 3 times, then leave under pressure for 1 hour. Remove from the bag and cut the radishes into irregular pieces with a small knife. Reserve in the brine until needed.

For the shiitake
Remove the stems from the mushrooms. Reserve the trimmings to make the mushroom and sansho powder.

In a hot saucepan, add a little olive oil and place half the mushrooms, with the tops facing down, and braise until they colour slightly. Then turn them over and do the same on the other sides. Season with salt, then deglaze with a little water so that it is soaked up by the mushrooms but also disappears almost immediately. For this dish, there is no need to cook the mushrooms any further.

With the remaining shiitakes, simply slice the mushrooms thinly so that all pieces have an equally thick cross-section. Allow 1 shiitake, cut into slices, per serving.

For the mushroom and sansho powder
Keep all the trim from shiitake preparations and dry in a dehydrator for 24 hours at 55°C (131°F) until super-crisp.

Once dry, process to a powder. Combine with sansho or lemon myrtle powder at a ratio of 1:1. →

Greens, per serve
6–8 young nasturtium leaves
6–8 sansho leaves

For the greens
Trim, wash and dry the leaves as needed, then portion.

To finish
Prepare a barbecue.

Brush the short rib portions with the glaze, then warm them over the barbecue. Allow the glaze to caramelize and take on the aroma of the charcoal.

Divide the braised shiitake into 4 portions and place 1 portion into each shallow serving bowl. Add the short rib next to it. Scatter over the radish pieces, pickled rock samphire and the slices of shiitake. Dust with a little mushroom and sansho powder, then scatter over the greens.

Raw scallop and roasted cauliflower, cured kelp and black truffle

For 4 people

Simple dashi
1.8 litres rainwater
60g dried kombu

Kelp cream and strips
reserved cooked kombu
  (see method)
100ml water
100g rendered pork fat
sea salt, to taste

Pine butter and pine buds
125g unsalted butter
20g young pine buds (available
  in the Otways during early
  spring only)

Cauliflower
4 slices of cauliflower, cut through
  as a vertical cross section,
  around 10cm in diameter and
  1.5cm thick
salt, to taste

Scallops
4 large hand-dived bay scallops
simple dashi (see above)
pine butter (see above)

To finish
lemon confit (see page 174)
5–6 slices of winter truffle per
  serve
pickled rock samphire
  (see page 196)
nasturtium leaves
10 lemon thyme leaves
purple flowering choi sum leaves
extra virgin black sesame oil
grated lemon zest

For the simple dashi
Combine the water and kombu in a vacuum pack and seal. Place the bag into a water bath set at 60°C (140°F) and leave to cook for 1 hour. Strain the contents and reserve the dashi and the kombu separately.

For the kelp cream and strips
Combine the reserved kombu with the water and pork fat and place the mixture in a vacuum pack. Braise the kombu at 80°C (176°F) for 12 hours. Once broken down and soft, remove a little of the kombu for cutting into 10cm × 2mm strips (2 per plate), then purée the remaining mixture to a smooth paste. Season with sea salt and reserve in a sealed container.

For the pine butter
Warm the butter in a saucepan over a medium heat until it starts to foam and begins to turn golden. Add the pine buds and gently sauté for 30 seconds or until you can smell the butter browning, along with the aroma of pine. Remove from the heat and chill rapidly so as not to overcook the pine buds or brown the butter too much. Reserve each product separately.

For the cauliflower
Preheat the oven to 140°C (285°F).
  Sear the cut sides of the cauliflower to an even golden colour on a plancha, then transfer them to a baking tray. Season well with salt and cover with both baking paper and kitchen (aluminum) foil. Roast for approximate 6–8 minutes until the cauliflower is still al dente but not crunchy or raw. Chill rapidly until required.

For the scallops
Shuck the scallops and remove them from the shells. Remove the skirt, muscle, roe and any impurities. Rinse the scallops quickly in the reserved dashi to ensure there is no fine sand or grit left on them. Slice each scallop into 3–4 pieces and brush each piece with some pine butter.

To serve
Warm a little pine butter in a saucepan, then roll the cauliflower in the foaming butter until warm. Add the reserved pine buds, a little confit lemon and the kombu strips and gently braise everything for a few minutes so that the flavours mingle together.
  In the centre of each serving bowl, place a heaped teaspoonful of the kombu paste and then cover it with 3–4 pieces of raw scallop. Place the cauliflower over the top, then spoon over the pine butter and other ingredients in the pan. Shave a little black truffle over the top and scatter with the nasturtium, samphire, lemon thyme and purple choi leaves. Microplane over a little lemon zest for freshness and drizzle a good amount of black sesame oil on and around the other ingredients.

Striped trumpeter and cured pork, butter-braised turnip and walnut

For 4 people

Fermented cucumber skin powder
3 cucumbers
sea salt

Pork fat
1 piece of cured pork back fat
  weighing approximately 100g

Turnip
1 large (baseball-size) Japanese
  or golden turnip
100g unsalted butter
25ml shiro (white) soy sauce
100ml water
salt, to taste

Walnut cream
130g walnuts
olive oil
3.75g rapadura sugar
37.5ml shiro (white) soy sauce
8.5ml mirin
8.5ml sake, with the alcohol
  burnt off
5.5ml water
0.25g gellan gum
salt, to taste
Note – these quantities yield
enough for 10 serves

Striped trumpeter
1 × 3kg whole striped trumpeter
salt, to taste
olive oil

Shaved walnut
8 walnuts

For the fermented cucumber skin powder

Peel 2 of the cucumbers. Follow the method for making fermented cucumber skin powder on page 142, but leave the vacuum-packed cucumbers at room temperature to ferment for around 3 weeks rather than 10 days.

Peel the remaining cucumbers. Transfer the skins to a dehydrator and dehydrate at 55°C (131°F) until completely dry. Process the skins to a powder using either a spice grinder or a mortar and pestle. Reserve in an airtight container until required.

For the finished powder, make a mixture of the 2 powders using a ratio of 75 per cent fermented skins powder to 25 per cent dried skins powder. Reserve in an airtight container.

For the pork fat

Slice the cured back fat into thin rectangular slices using a meat slicer – aim for slices that measure roughly 7cm × 12.5cm. Store the slices between sheets of greaseproof (wax) paper.

For the turnip

Using a Japanese circular slicer, cut long ribbons from the turnip, leaving the ribbons as wide as the turnip (roughly 7cm) and cutting the lengths down to around 15cm.

In a saucepan, whisk the butter, soy sauce and water together over a medium heat until an emulsion forms, season to taste, then bring it to the boil. Pour the mixture over the turnip ribbons and leave to cool, allowing the turnip to cook. As soon as the ribbons are cooked to the desired stage (they should remain crisp and not be falling apart), chill them immediately to prevent overcooking. Leave the turnip ribbons in the emulsion until required.

For the walnut cream

Gently brown the walnuts in a wide-based pan with a little oil over a medium heat. Stir continuously so as not to burn any part of the walnuts.

Once the nuts take on a deep golden colour, remove them from the heat and pat dry to absorb any excess oil. Combine the walnuts with the remaining ingredients, except the salt, and process in a food processor to a smooth paste.

Heat the walnut mixture to 95°C (203°F) to activate the gellan gum, then leave to cool in a refrigerator over several hours. Once cold and the gellan has hardened the walnut paste, return the mixture to a food processor and process to a smooth cream. It may split a little as the natural oil in the nuts start to heat up – if this happens,
add a touch more water to bring it back. Season to taste and reserve, refrigerated, until needed.

For the striped trumpeter

Prepare a barbecue.

Head, gut and fillet the fish, then remove the pin bones. Next, remove the skin, then carefully separate the top loins along the sinew/fillet line into 3 loins. Separate the fillets into 45g portions, taking the portions by cutting across the grain of the fillet.

Seal the fish on the skin side, then let it 'fall over' onto the plancha to sear the widest side, giving it some colour but not cooking the piece through. This side will be the cooking side. Transfer the trumpeter to the barbecue and roast the fish over charcoal until medium rare – do not turn the fish so that it gets a type of roasted crust on one side and has a soft, almost rare texture on the other. Season to taste with salt and brush with olive oil.

For the shaved walnuts

Peel the nuts and remove the inner membrane to separate each nut into 2 halves. Using a truffle slicer or mandoline, shave the nuts into fine slices. Allow 2g per serve.

To serve

Warm the pork fat to at least an ambient temperature so that it is translucent and cover it with the cucumber powder.

Warm the turnips in their emulsion. Place a small pile of shaved walnuts in the centre of each shallow serving bowl and drape a turnip ribbon over it, spooning a little of the emulsion over for moisture. Place the fish over the turnip, add the walnut cream just below and drape the pork fat over the fish.

This morning, this spring

There are times of the year when the garden really pushes the menu and assists my creative process in a way that can make me question if I'm in charge of the direction we're heading in or merely just another life force existing symbiotically with all the other energies sharing space on this hillside. Winter is quite the opposite – reserves come into play, both with produce and creativity. It can be bleak and lean. 'Green cuisine' is what I call the food we serve in winter and early spring, due to the lack of colour variation on the plate and in the sky and garden before the weather and life cycle change. In winter we have to be more reliant on ideas started in summer and produce prepared and put away for this less-productive time. But spring is spontaneous, and as I've mentioned before, if you are in the right spot and allow yourself to be open to possibilities without overthinking, and more importantly, suggestion, spring can be an amazing time to be a cook with a garden.

This morning, this spring is a dish that intends to mimick the experience of being in the garden, picking when the season breaks but the mornings still crunch with ice, when flowers tell us of the changes occurring, and when energy levels creep back into the kitchen. It's cold, out picking for the day in this weather, but the plants and soil are already warmer than the week before, and the new life everywhere feels warm.

This morning, this spring: first asparagus, peas, frozen radish

For 4 people

Asparagus
4 freshly picked asparagus spears
salt
lemon-pressed olive oil

Pistachio purée
250g pistachios
25ml olive oil

Chlorophyll and pistachio
approximately 300g spinach
25g pistachio purée
10ml olive oil
1g dried sansho pepper
salt, to taste

Frozen radish
450g daikon
300g fennel
150g cucumber
20ml mirin
1.875g salt
approximately 2 lovage leaves,
    julienned

Peas and radish flowers
32 pea flowers
32 watermelon radish flowers

To serve
sansho powder
freeze-dried sake powder
lemon-pressed olive oil

For the asparagus
With a sharp turning knife and starting just below the head of the asparagus, peel the first fibre off each piece. It is important to peel in one motion from top to bottom, ensuring you do not peel too deeply or scratch the stems. Blanch the peeled asparagus spears in boiling salted water with a ratio of 10g salt per 1 litre water. Refresh it in heavily iced water. The asparagus should be just cooked with a little crunch. Once completely cold, remove the asparagus from the ice bath, dry it and trim the woody end from each piece, making a each spear. Season with a little salt and lemon-pressed olive oil and store, covered, until service.

For the pistachio purée
Combine the pistachios with the olive oil and place the mixture in a Pacojet canister. Freeze the pistachios, then Pacotize to a smooth paste. (The Pacojet is very useful for puréeing nuts as it produces a very smooth paste.)

For the chlorophyll and pistachio
Wash the spinach and process it in a juicer. Place the spinach juice in a saucepan and heat it, stirring constantly, to 70°C (158°F). At this temperature the solid chlorophyll will separate from the water. Pass the juice through a fine sieve (strainer), discarding the liquid and keeping the solid chlorophyll left in the strainer. It may need to be dried by spreading it over absorbent paper. Reserve 50g of this spinach chlorophyll.
  Combine the chlorophyll and pistachio purée at a ratio of 2 parts chlorophyll to 1 part pistachio, then add the sansho powder and a little olive oil. Season to taste. Store in an airtight container until needed. This purée has a shelf-life of 2 days.

For the frozen radish
Juice all the vegetables separately, then pass the individual juices through a fine sieve (strainer). Combine 300g daikon juice with 180g fennel juice and 100g cucumber juice, then add the mirin and salt. Freeze the juice mixture to at least −20°C (−4°F), then pass the ice through a mouli to achieve a granita texture. Fold through the lovage leaves and 'fluff' the mixture with a fork. Reserve, frozen, until needed.

For the pea and radish flowers
Using scissors, cut the flowers from their respective plants. When washing them, ensure that it is done quickly in iced water, taking special care not to damage the fragile petals on the radish flowers. Pat each flower dry with absorbent paper, allowing 8 of each flower per plate. Store them, refrigerated, in airtight containers until needed.

To serve
On each flat serving plate, drag a tablespoonful of the pistachio purée down the middle, then sprinkle a little sansho powder over the top. Lay 1 asparagus spear down the right side of the purée and scatter the flowers to the left. Sprinkle some freeze-dried sake over the asparagus and drizzle a little lemon oil over the plate and other ingredients. Add a large spoonful of the frozen radish to the right of the asparagus and serve.

Tomatoes and uncommon leaves in sea water

For 4 people

Tomatoes
6–8 large sun-ripened heirloom
  tomatoes
sea salt, to taste
olive oil

Sea water
900g mussels
650ml water
xanthan gum
grated lemon zest

Tomato vinaigrette
500g tomato pulp or roughly
  chopped sun-ripened tomatoes
5g caster sugar
1g salt
500ml Arbequina olive oil
salt, to taste

Leaves
a good mix of ice plant, red and
  green orach, red vein sorrel,
  small lovage, minutina buds,
  pickled nasturtium buds, and
  golden purslane leaves, allowing
  8–12 of each type of leaf per
  portion

Flowers
10 garlic chive flowers or
  5 coriander flowers (depending
  on the season) per serve

For the tomatoes
Slice each tomato into even slices with a thickness of around 1.5cm. Transfer to a tray, season with sea salt and leave at room temperature for approximately 1 hour so that the salt begins to draw out the moisture in the tomato.

Preheat the oven to 65°C (149°F). Cover the tomato slices with olive oil and leave in the preheated oven to confit for around 30–45 minutes, or until the tomato appears to be more cooked than raw. When you are happy with how they are, remove them from the oven and leave to slowly cool to room temperature.

For the sea water
Scrub the mussels with steel wool, ensuring that all barnacles and grit are completely removed, and rinse the mussels in fresh water. Place them in a saucepan with the water. Place a lid on the pan and, over a low heat, bring the liquid to a very gentle simmer. Allow the stock to simmer for around 40 minutes and for the juices from the mussels to combine and cook with the water.

Strain the resulting liquid through a fine sieve (strainer) and chill it rapidly. Add xanthan gum at a ratio of 3g xanthan per 1 litre liquid, then lemon zest to taste.

For the tomato vinaigrette
Combine the tomato pulp with the sugar and salt. Roughly crush the pulp by hand, then place it in a saucepan and cover with the oil. Cook the tomato slowly over a low heat for around 1 hour, ensuring the temperature never goes above 65°C (149°F). Once cooked, pass the mixture through a mouli and season the resulting vinaigrette to taste.

For the leaves
Cut the leaves to the desired sizes – aim for a variety of sizes, but keep them relevant to the size of the dish and the plate being used to present it. Nothing should be larger than around 10cm. Wash the leaves in iced water and portion them into 4 even portions.

To serve
Divide the tomatoes into 4 portions. Arrange each portion on a serving plate with the leaves and flowers. Dress everything with the sea water and drizzle the vinaigrette over the sea water so that it beads rather than emulsifies.

Tomatoes and mussels gently braised in sea butter

For 4 people

Tomatoes
40 small tomatoes of varying sizes
 and varieties
salt, to taste
olive oil

Tomato vinaigrette
500g tomatoes
5g caster sugar
1g salt, plus extra to taste
20ml Arbequina olive oil
12ml aged Moscatel vinegar
about 20g finely chopped chives
salt, to taste
0.5g xanthan gum

Mussels
1kg large blue mussels

Sea butter
100g unsalted butter
4g sea lettuce powder
sea salt, to taste

Mussel butter
125g cold unsalted butter
175g mussel meat
1.5g lemon myrtle powder
1.5g anise myrtle powder
finely Microplaned zest of 1
 Tahitian lime

Soured shallots
200g shallots
5 large sprigs of summer savory
6–10 mountain peppercorns
200ml olive oil
12ml Cabernet Sauvignon vinegar
12ml barrel-aged mirin
salt, to taste

**Herbs, leaves and flowers,
per serve**
5 small nasturtium buds
 and stems
5 varying sized leaves of golden
 purslane
5 olive plant leaves
4 stems of pickled rock samphire
 (see page 196)
10 garlic chive flowers or
5 coriander flowers (depending
 on the season)

For the tomatoes

The larger tomatoes need to be blanched, refreshed, peeled and then dried in a dehydrator at 55°C (131°F) for 12 hours. Allow 2 dried tomatoes per serve. This partial dehydration intensifies the umami quality of the tomatoes, creating a rich, deep flavour, and provides an interesting, almost chewy texture.

Preheat the oven to 80°C (176°F).

Blanch the smaller tomatoes (8 per serve), then peel them and spread them out on a baking tray. Season with salt and coat lightly with olive oil. Dry them in the oven for 1 hour.

Once both sizes of tomatoes are dried, they can be portioned together and left at room temperature.

For the tomato vinaigrette

Combine the tomatoes with the sugar and salt. Roughly crush the pulp by hand into a bowl, really massaging the ingredients together. Put the mixture into a fine cloth or fine conical sieve and leave it to hang for around 6 hours to filter the juice.

Once completely drained, combine 160ml of the strained tomato water with the olive oil and vinegar and season if necessary. Mix in the xanthan gum. Add the chives – the vinaigrette should be quite laden with chives. Reserve the vinaigrette in an airtight container, refrigerated, until needed.

For the mussels

To open the mussels, put them into a saucepan and cover with cold water. Place over a medium heat and gently warm. Remove the mussels one by one as they open. Reserve and chill a little of the poaching liquor.

While the mussels are still warm, remove the beards, then remove the mussels from the shells. Store the shucked mussels in the chilled poaching liquor.

For the sea butter

Combine the softened butter and sea lettuce and work together until the sea lettuce powder is evenly distributed. Season to taste with sea salt and reserve until required. This butter will keep, refrigerated, for around 1 week, but can be frozen for longer.

For the mussel butter

Combine 50g of the butter with the mussels and process on a high speed setting in a food processor until the mussels are completely broken down. Pass this mixture through a fine sieve (strainer), then combine it with the remaining ingredients, except the salt, working them to a homogenous paste. Season to taste, then store refrigerated. Given that this butter contains shellfish, it has a short shelf-life and should be used within 3 days.

Soured shallots

Peel the shallots, then slice them into even thin rounds. Use a skewer or similar to poke out the eye of the shallot so that all rings are separate and there an no traces of the yellow or root/core of the shallot. Place the shallot rings in a saucepan, add the summer savory and pepper and cover with the oil. On a low heat, gently simmer the shallots until al dente. Remove from the heat, stir in the vinegars and season with salt. Let the shallots cool in the oil, then transfer everything to an airtight container. These can keep for some time refrigerated under oil.

For the herbs, leaves and flowers

Wash the leaves, refresh them in ice, then dry the leaves on absorbent paper. Portion them together, keeping the pickled rock samphire separately as the acids will cook the fresh leaves. Store in the refrigerator until ready to serve.

To serve

Warm equal parts of both butters together in a saucepan, add the tomatoes and gently coat with the butters. The butter mixture should not split and the tomatoes should remain whole or as intact as possible. Add the mussels and continue to fold the ingredients onto themselves so that everything is coated in the butters. Season with salt to taste.

In each serving bowl, arrange the tomatoes and then the mussels and place 5 rings of soured shallot over the top. Dress everything with the tomato vinaigrette and scatter over the leaves and flowers.

Recipes

Wild mushrooms

Each year, as autumn approaches in the Otways, but before the chilled air and frosted nights have cooled the soil too much, we get a good season for edible wild mushrooms. We are lucky that, within 15–20 minutes of the restaurant, we can pretty much pick all we need, with kilos of pristine mushrooms available.

There are, of course, thousands of different types of fungi growing in Australia, most of them highly toxic to humans and certainly not edible. But there are a few varieties growing on the edge of, or within pine plantations, which provide the necessary symbiotic conditions for edible mushrooms to flourish that are not native.

Given the risks associated with gathering wild fungi, we limit our foraging to two main varieties that we know well and that provide great culinary value. Actually, the more time I spend foraging for mushrooms, the less interested I've become in wanting to try different varieties and, of course, there are so many 'look-alike' species that it's almost impossible to tell the difference between something edible and something toxic, even if using the limited field guides that exist on this subject in Australia, so we just stick to what we know.

My favourite, and one that grows early in the season, relying on humidity and warmer soil to exist in this region, is the slippery jack. A member of the Boletus family, it has a slippery cap and, when larger, can deteriorate quite quickly in wet conditions. We find that, on warmer days after good rain, these mushrooms grow quickly. The best specimens are picked when the heads are around 5cm in diameter. Of course, they grow much larger and, for drying to an intense powder for seasoning, these are great, but if we can get them on their first day of growth and pick them small, before their slimy characteristic has developed, they are an incredible flavour bomb and their firm texture makes them ideal to serve raw.

Pine mushrooms or saffron milk caps are found later in the season (although there is a time when these varieties overlap) and are probably more prolific. Orange in colour and quite woody as they grow in size, they are a hardier mushroom and benefit from cooking because they tend to have a bitter note later in the season, as the weather cools and they age. On their own, they do not make a particularly good dried powder, but they can be added to dried slippery jacks to give a real pine forest flavour, as they tend to have more of this flavour profile.

Wild mushrooms and milk curd, chicken liver and chicken broth

For 4 people

Pine oil
500ml olive oil
10 sprigs of thyme
25g fresh pine needles
25g dried pine needles
10 black peppercorns,
   lightly crushed
5g garlic clove, cracked open
50g pine mushrooms

Roast chicken broth
5kg chicken frames
400g white onions
250g carrots
3.5kg chicken wings
olive oil
20g truffle trim, finely diced

Curds and whey
1 litre biodynamic cow's milk
30ml white vinegar

Dried liver
150g chicken livers
250ml water
250ml milk
2.5g salt
anchovy fish sauce
500ml sunflower oil
20g cocoa nibs, finely shaved
   with a Microplane
10g lime zest

Mushrooms
40g each of small to medium-
   sized slippery jack and pine
   mushrooms
pine oil (see above)

Pasta
250g whole wheat
(wholemeal) flour
2 whole eggs
3 egg yolks
olive oil

For the pine oil
Combine all the ingredients in a saucepan and bring to 80°C (176°F). Leave to infuse at this temperature for around 1 hour. Leave to stand at room temperature for at least 24 hours. Strain off the solids and reserve the oil.

For the roast chicken broth
First make a white chicken stock. Peel and cut the vegetables into large, even dice. Put them into a saucepan with the chicken frames, cover with water and simmer gently for 4–6 hours, skimming regularly.
   While the chicken stock is cooking, joint the wings, dress them evenly in olive oil and seal them in a hot pan to a deep golden brown colour. Remove any excess fat from the wings with absorbent paper.
   Strain the white chicken stock and combine it with the chicken wings. Simmer for 4 hours until a rich brown chicken broth is achieved. Strain a couple of times through a fine sieve (strainer) and chill immediately.
   Add the finely chopped truffle to this broth at service time.

For the curds and whey
Follow the recipe for ricotta on page 220 to make the curds and whey. Reserve the curds for this recipe and the whey for other dishes.

For the dried liver
To clean the livers, remove any sinew, outer membrane and fat and make a small cut in each end. Vacuum pack with the water, milk and salt and poach in a water bath for 3 hours at 40°C (104°F). Strain the livers, dry them and then marinate for 30 minutes in the fish sauce at a ratio of 20 per cent fish sauce per weight of liver.
   Remove the livers from the marinade and pat them dry. Place them in a saucepan with the sunflower oil and gently heat to 140°C (285°F). Hold this temperature for around 15 minutes or until the livers are completely cooked and slightly dehydrated, but not fried.
   Remove the livers from the oil, pat them dry of any excess oil and pulse them in a food processor until torn into a floss. Combine 100g liver floss with the finely shaved cocoa nibs and lime zest. Store in an airtight container.

For the mushrooms
Given that mushrooms are served raw in this dish, they need to be of very high quality, picked on the day of serving and cleaned correctly. Brush the tops with a mushroom brush or knife and ensure that there is no grit or any insects underneath the tops. The slippery jacks have a delicious stem, so use these, but the pine mushrooms should have their stems removed.
   Reserve the mushrooms under an ever-so-slightly damp cloth until required.
   Put the pine oil into a saucepan, add the whole pine mushrooms from the selection, bring gently to 80°C (176°F) and cook for around 20 minutes or until the mushrooms are cooked.

For the pasta
Combine the flour and eggs and knead for 10 minutes until the dough is glossy and the gluten is developed. Wrap in clingfilm (plastic wrap) and leave to rest for at least 1 hour.
   Roll out the dough using a pasta machine set to number 1. Cut into 4–5cm-wide ribbons on the diagonal to create a type of pasta sheet. Blanch until just cooked in boiling salted water, then dress with olive oil and divide into 4 portions.

To finish
Place 1 tablespoon curd on each serving plate and drape 1 portion of pasta ribbons over. Add the whole confit pine mushroom and then a spoonful of dried liver over the plated ingredients. Cut the mushrooms into quarters and scatter these over the dish before pouring in the warm chicken broth.

Wild mushrooms and pasture-raised Wagyu, buckwheat and black garlic

For 4 people

Black garlic
whole heads of garlic

Fermented buckwheat
35g salt
1.4 litres water at room
   temperature
600g buckwheat
salt, to taste

Pine oil
500ml olive oil
10 sprigs of thyme
25g fresh pine needles
25g dried pine needles
10 black peppercorns,
   lightly crushed
5g garlic clove, cracked open
50g pine mushrooms

Mushrooms
120g selection of small to
   medium-sized slippery jack
   and pine mushrooms

Beef
rack of 2 short ribs from pasture-
   raised Wagyu beef or similar

Veal stock
10kg veal knuckle bones
olive oil
8kg stewing beef
1.6kg large carrots
3.7kg brown onions
650g large, ripe tomatoes
25 litres water
1 pork trotter
½ calf's foot, split
Note – these quantities yield more
stock than is required for this
recipe but this is a minimum
amount to make →

For the black garlic
To ferment the garlic, wrap the whole heads tightly in several layers of kitchen (aluminum) foil and place in a dehydrator. Dehydrate at 55°C (131°F) for around 5 weeks or until the cloves turn a deep caramelized black colour and have a chewy texture. Separate the cloves and dehydrate them a little further until hard. Process to a fine powder. Save in an airtight container or under vacuum until needed.

For the buckwheat
Dissolve the salt in the water. Combine the buckwheat with the brine in a sterilized 2-litre preserving jar and seal tightly. Leave at room temperature for at least 3 weeks.

Remove the buckwheat from the jar and blanch it in boiling water for no more than 1 minute. Season to taste, drain the buckwheat and chill it rapidly so as to avoid any over cooking.

For the pine oil
Combine all the ingredients in a saucepan and bring to 80°C (176°F). Leave to infuse at this temperature for around 1 hour. Remove from the heat and leave to stand at room temperature for at least 24 hours. Strain off the solids and reserve the oil.

For the mushrooms
Given that mushrooms are served raw in this dish, they need to be of very high quality, picked on the day of serving and cleaned correctly. Brush the tops with a mushroom brush or knife and ensure that there is no grit or any insects underneath the tops. The slippery jacks have a delicious stem, so use these, but the pine mushrooms should have their stems removed.

Reserve the mushrooms under an ever-so-slightly damp cloth until required.

For the beef
Wrap the piece of beef in kitchen (aluminum) foil so that the bones do not puncture the vacuum pack and then seal in a vacuum pack on maximum pressure. Place the short rib into a water bath and cook for 24 hours at 72°C (162°F).

After this time, when the meat is soft, remove the short rib and, while hot, slide the bones out. Leave the meat to cool and firm up.

Cut the meat into rectangular portions of around 25g. Place the portions in a vacuum pack once more so that they can be warmed for service.

For the veal stock
Preheat the oven to 200°C (390°F).

Rub the veal bones with oil and roast them to a deep golden, turning them as necessary and draining off excessive amounts of fat.

Cut the beef into large pieces, coat it with oil and roast to a deep brown.

Peel the carrots and onions. Roast the carrots whole. Halve the onions and roast them until dark.

Halve the tomatoes and roast them until dark in colour.

Place all roasted ingredients into a large stockpot with the remaining ingredients and bring to a gentle simmer. Skim any fat and impurities from the surface and simmer for 12 hours. Ensure the stock never boils hard and skim it regularly during the cooking time.

Once the stock has cooked for the prescribed time, pass it first through a coarse sieve (strainer), then a fine one, then return it to the stove to reduce. Continue to skim any impurities from the surface and reduce the liquid to 5 litres.

Pass the stock once again through a fine strainer and cool rapidly. Reserve until needed. →

Glaze
100g shallots
20g ginger
25ml Japanese sesame oil
2g red Szechuan pepper
50g maple syrup
100ml sake
400g eel meat and bones
2.5 litres veal stock (see
page 216)
salt, to taste

Aubergine (eggplant) and white
miso purée
1 large aubergine (eggplant)
400ml water
15ml light soy sauce
5g caster sugar
4g salt
gellan gum
Marinade:
1 garlic clove
125g shiro (white) miso
60ml light soy sauce
30ml lemon juice
10ml pure or white Japanese
sesame oil
100ml aubergine cooking liquor

For the glaze
Slice the shallots and ginger.
Warm the sesame oil in a wide saucepan and slowly sweat the shallots and ginger without colouring. Add the Szechuan pepper, then the maple syrup and allow to lightly caramelize.
Deglaze with the sake. Add the eel, then the veal stock. Bring the stock to a gentle simmer and cook out slowly, skimming impurities that surface. Reduce the stock as it cooks to 750ml. Pass it through a fine sieve (strainer), season to taste and chill rapidly.

For the aubergine (eggplant) and white miso purée
Peel away the aubergine (eggplant) skin, then cut the flesh into smaller, equal-sized pieces. Blanch the aubergine pieces in the water combined with the soy sauce, sugar and salt, keeping them submerged with a cartouche or similar. The aubergine should simmer for 8–10 minutes to ensure that it is completely cooked.
Meanwhile, prepare the marinade. Mince the garlic and combine it with all the remaining marinade ingredients to form a homogenous paste.
Once the aubergine is cooked through, remove the pieces from the cooking liquor and combine it with the marinade at a ratio of 400g blanched aubergine to 100g marinade. Purée the mixture and allow to cool.
When the mixture is completely cold, transfer it to a Thermomix and thicken with a ratio of 0.5g gellan gum to 100g purée.

To finish
Prepare a barbecue.
Warm the short rib portions over the barbecue, brushing the pieces with the glaze and allowing it to caramelize.
Warm the aubergine and white miso purée. Combine some of the buckwheat with some of the veal stock and bring to a gentle simmer.
Slice the mushrooms into thin, even slices, maintaining a cross section of each mushroom. Dress with a little pine oil before warming the mushrooms slightly under a salamander or grill (broiler).
Place 1 tablespoon of the warmed aubergine and white miso purée on each serving plate, then a portion of the short rib. Cover with a tablespoonful of the buckwheat and veal stock mixture, then the slices of mushrooms. Using.a fine sieve (strainer), dust the black garlic powder liberally over the top.

Warm ricotta and nettle, winter truffle and brassicas

For 4 people

Dried brassicas
a sizeable mixture of any of the
following: Empress of India,
nasturtium, Red Russian kale,
broad leaf mustard, Osaka
mustard, cavolo nero, kohlrabi
leaf, kai lan, shaved cauliflower
salt, to taste

Dried brassica and mushroom powders
dried brassicas (see above)
mushrooms – use a mixture of
equal parts of slippery jack, pine
and shiitake mushrooms
Note – use quantities that are
large enough to allow the blades
of your food processor to cut the
ingredients

Leek ash
2 medium-sized leeks, such as
Jaune du Poitou or King Richard
olive oil
Note - This yields more than
is needed, but is a minimum
amount to be practical to
process when dry

Winter truffle
20g Australian winter truffle

Ricotta
1 litre biodynamic cow's milk
30ml white vinegar

Nettle paste
150g blanched nettle leaves
20ml reserved whey (see method)
ricotta (see above)
salt, to taste

Roast chicken broth
400g white onions
250g carrots
5kg chicken frames
3.5kg chicken wings
olive oil
truffle trim (see above), finely diced

Chicken skin
skin from 1 chicken
sea salt, to taste

For the dried brassicas
Blanch the more robust leaves, then refresh them and dry them on absorbent paper. Tender leaves can go straight into the dehydrator. Dehydrate the prepared leaves at 55°C (131°F) for around 4–6 hours (but up to 12) or until completely crisp. It is imperative that the leaves have a real crunch to give this dish some textural interest. Once dry, allow 8–10 pieces of assorted brassica leaves per serve, reserving the rest to make the dried brassica powder. Ensure that all leaves are seasoned thoroughly.

For the dried brassica and mushroom powders
To make the brassica powder, process the dried brassicas on a high speed setting in a food processor and sift away any bits that are not fully dried. Store in an airtight container.

To make the mushroom powder, clean the mushrooms, then dehydrate at 55°C (131°F) for 24–36 hours until completely dry. Process the mushrooms to a powder in a food processor and sift out larger or undried pieces. Store in an airtight container.

For the leek ash
Prepare a barbecue.

Remove the outer leaves from the leeks and dress them in olive oil. Lightly grill over charcoal, then leave them to dry overnight using residual heat in the masonry oven.

When dry, process the leeks to a fine powder. Reserve in an airtight container.

For the truffle
Using a toothbrush, mushroom brush or similar, dust off any dirt left on the truffle. Slice into ultra-fine, nice rounds, allowing 3–5g per serve. Reserve any bits that break away from the truffle or end pieces that do not slice well, and chop them finely, for the truffle trim to add to the chicken broth when serving. Ensure that the truffle is served at room temperature.

For the ricotta
Warm the milk to 80°C (176°F), then add the vinegar and gently stir while increasing the heat to 85°C (185°F). Allow the curds to separate. Remove the milk from the heat and allow it to cool to room temperature. Strain the whey from the curds and reserve the whey and curd/ricotta separately.

For the nettle paste and ricotta
Combine the nettle leaves and 20g of the reserved whey in a Thermomix and process on a high speed setting at 50°C (122°F) until well combined. Pass the mixture through a fine chinois and combine with the ricotta at a ratio of 1 part nettle paste to 3 parts ricotta to achieve a green, nettle-flavoured ricotta. Season to taste.

For the roast chicken broth
First make a white chicken stock. Peel and cut the vegetables into large, even dice. Put them into a saucepan with the chicken frames, cover with water and simmer gently for 4–6 hours, skimming regularly.

While the chicken stock is cooking, joint the wings, dress them evenly in olive oil and seal them in a hot pan to a deep golden brown colour. Remove any excess fat from the wings with absorbent paper.

Strain the white chicken stock and combine it with the chicken wings. Simmer for 4 hours until a rich brown chicken broth is achieved. Strain a couple of times through a fine sieve (strainer) and chill immediately.

Add the reserved finely chopped truffle to this broth at service.

For the chicken skin
Preheat the oven to 150°C (302°F).

Scrape any fat from the inside of the skin, taking care not to tear it. Place the skin between sheets of baking paper and place between 2 heavy baking sheets. Place a weight on the top tray to keep the skin flat and bake for approximately 1 hour. The skin should come out only when it is crisp, glassy and golden.

Season with sea salt. Dry the skin on absorbent paper and leave to cool. Once cooled, break the skin into smaller pieces. Allow 4 pieces per serve.

To serve
Warm the ricotta and divide it between 4 serving bowls, placing a large tablespoonful in the centre of each. Sprinkle a pinch of each of the 3 powders over the ricotta, then stick the brassicas and chicken skin into the ricotta so all the leaves are standing upright. Ensure the leaves and skin push through the ricotta all the way to the surface of the bowl so that they do not fall over. Scatter the truffle slices over the top and amongst the leaves, then pour the hot broth around the ricotta.

Watermelon, quandongs, rhubarb and rose

For 4 people

Rhubarb stock syrup
500g rhubarb
250g caster sugar
1 litre water

Watermelon
3–4 slices from a large
watermelon
rhubarb stock syrup (see above)

Quandong
6 quandongs
approximately 50ml rhubarb
  stock syrup (see above)

Roasted beetroot purée
150g Bull's Blood beetroot (beets)
  or other similarly dark beetroot

Burnt beetroot custard
Makes enough to fill
½ gastronorm pan
150g egg yolks
100g caster sugar
225ml milk
1 vanilla bean, seeds scraped
135g roasted beetroot (beets)
purée
540ml cream
3g gold leaf gelatine, soaked

Poached green juniper
25g caster sugar
100ml water
5 lemon verbena leaves
50 green juniper berries

Rhubarb and rose granita
400g rhubarb
25ml water
22.5g caster sugar
10ml rose water
1.5g salt

Snow pea juice
200g snow peas (mangetout)
xanthan gum
salt, to taste

Leaves, per serve
several small leaves of mixed
  mints and lemon balm

For the rhubarb stock syrup
Follow the instructions on page 136
to make the rhubarb stock syrup.

For the watermelon
Cut 1cm-thick slices of watermelon across
the fruit. Using a pastry cutter with a
diameter of 4–5cm, cut out 12 rounds of
watermelon. Place these in a vacuum bag
with twice their weight of rhubarb stock.
Compress with maximum pressure and
leave to infuse for 2–3 hours.

For the quandong
Cut each quandong in half. Combine the
halves with the rhubarb stock syrup. Place
in a vacuum bag and cook at 60°C (140°F)
for 30 minutes. Chill the quandong rapidly,
then strain the liquid from the quandongs
and reduce it by half. Reserve the quandongs in the reduced liquid.

For the roasted beetroot purée
Preheat the oven to 140°C (285°F). Wrap
the whole beetroots (beets) in kitchen
(aluminum) foil and bake for around 1 hour.
Once cooked and still warm, rub the skins
off the beetroot and process them on high
speed in a food processor.

For the burnt beetroot custard
Preheat the oven to 160°C (320°C).
  In a bowl, whisk together the egg yolks
and sugar. Combine the milk and vanilla
seeds in a saucepan and bring to the boil,
then pour the milk over the egg and sugar
mixture. Transfer the mixture to a saucepan
set over a medium heat and stir slowly but
continuously until the mixture reaches
82°C (180°F).
  Whisk the beetroot (beets) purée and
cream into the custard and transfer the
mixture to a deep baking tray. Bake for
20–30 minutes, until the surface of the
custard turns a deep golden colour – this
caramelisation is imperative to the outcome
of the custard, as it provides the 'burnt'
flavour. Once the desired colour is achieved
and the custard has separated, appearing
curdled, remove it from the oven and
transfer to a food processor together with
the hydrated gelatine. Process the mixture
on a high speed setting for 2–3 minutes
until it has a smooth, velvety texture. When
smooth, and with the aid of a confectionery
funnel, transfer the mixture into a piping
(pastry) bag. Keep refrigerated until needed.

For the poached green juniper
Dissolve the sugar in the water, add the
verbena and then the juniper. Simmer
gently until the syrup thickens slightly
and the juniper softens.

For the rhubarb and rose granita
Juice the rhubarb to obtain 200ml rhubarb
juice. Combine the juice with the remaining ingredients and stir to dissolve the
sugar. Freeze the mixture, forking it every
20 minutes or so to obtain a granita.
Reserve in a sealed container in the
freezer until needed.

For the snow pea juice
Juice the snow peas (mangetout) several
times so that all possible juice is extracted.
Pass the juice through a fine sieve
(strainer) and then leave to stand for
around 1 hour to allow the starch to settle
on the bottom.
  Carefully decant the juice, leaving behind
the starch. Thicken 100ml of the juice with
xanthan gum at a ratio of 3g per litre of
juice. Season with a little salt.

For the leaves
Trim the stems off the leaves so they all
have clean ends. Wash the leaves in iced
water. Reserve the leaves and flowers
on damp paper in a sealed container
until service.

To finish
Drizzle around 1 tablespoon of snow pea
juice into the centre of each serving bowl,
then fill the quandong halves with the
beetroot custard and arrange them over
the pea juice along with the watermelon
rounds (3 per serve). Scatter over 5–6
juniper berries and then dust over the top
a large spoonful of the granita. Quickly add
the mint and lemon balm leaves before the
granita melts and serve.

Milk and honey, mandarin and black truffle

For 4 people

Sheep's milk ice cream
(for 1 Pacojet canister)
25g caster sugar
1.3g sorbet neutral emulsifier/
  stabilizer
150g sheep's milk
75g sheep's milk yogurt
150ml water
30g milk powder
70g dextrose
35g trimoline

Honeycomb
80g caster sugar
12.5g honey
31g glucose
15ml water
3.5g bicarbonate of soda
  (baking soda), sifted

Milk crumble
50g clarified butter
125g skimmed milk powder
7.5g chopped truffle
5g finely chopped honeycomb
  (see above)
12.5g finely chopped freeze-dried
  mandarin segments

Roasted milk skins
1 litre whole (full-fat) milk
50ml cream mixed with 25ml
  whole (full-fat) milk
icing (confectioners') sugar, to dust

Citrus stock syrup
2 mandarins
2 lemons
750g caster sugar
500ml water

Mandarin
5 Imperial mandarins (or a similar
  variety)
citrus stock syrup (see above)
gellan gum

Black truffle
4–5 slices of black truffle
  per serve

For the sheep's milk ice cream
Follow the instructions on page 228
to make the sheep's milk ice cream.

For the honeycomb
Combine the sugar, honey, glucose and
water in a saucepan and bring the mixture
to 153°C (307°F). Remove the pan from
the heat and whisk in the bicarbonate of
soda (baking soda). The mixture will bubble
rapidly. Pour onto a Silpat and allow to cool
and harden.
 Break the honeycomb into bite-sized
pieces. Store in an airtight container in the
freezer. Reserve 5g honeycomb, finely
chopped, separately in the freezer, to add
to the milk crumble.

For the milk crumble
Follow the instructions on page 228
to make the milk crumble. Mix 75g of the
crumble with the rest of the ingredients.

For the roasted milk skins
Follow the instructions on page 226 to
make the milk skins, only break down the
milk skins into pieces that are roughly
10cm X 3–4cm.

For the citrus stock syrup
Place the whole citrus fruit in a saucepan
and cover with water. Slowly bring the
water to a boil and blanch the fruit to
remove a little of the bitterness in the zest.
Leave to simmer for 2–3 minutes, then
remove the fruit from the heat and discard
the blanching water.
 Combine the sugar, water and the
blanched fruit in a saucepan and slowly
bring to a simmer over a low heat, allowing
the temperature of the water to climb to
105°C (221°F). Once this temperature is
reached, remove the saucepan from the
heat and leave the fruit to cool in the liquor.

For the mandarin
Peel and segment the mandarins and
remove any pith and seeds. Put the fruit
into a saucepan and cover with citrus stock
syrup. Bring to a gentle simmer and leave
to cook for around 15 minutes. After the
cooking time has elapsed, remove several
segments for the final plated dishes and
leave them to cool in some of the citrus
stock syrup.
 Remove any seeds that may be floating in
the cooking syrup and pass the remaining
fruit and syrup through a tamis to remove
any seeds that may have been missed.
Process the fruit and syrup in a food
processor until smooth, then combine the
mandarin purée with gellan gum at a ratio
of 3g to 450g fruit mixture.
 Heat the mixture to 90°C (194°F). Leave
to set and cool, then process to a smooth
gel in a food processor. Transfer to a piping
(pastry) bag and reserve, refrigerated.

To serve
Dust each plate with milk crumble, then
scatter over some large honeycomb
pieces. Place some of the mandarin gel to
the left side of the centre and a mandarin
segment to the right. Cover the gel with
3–4 milk skins per serve, layering slices of
black truffle between them. Place a scoop
of the ice cream as close as possible to
the skins.

Apricot and vanilla, sheep's milk and Brae farm honey

For 4 people

For the apricot stock
4 apricots, halved and kernels cracked
500ml water
375g caster sugar
seeds from ½ vanilla bean
Note – these quantities yield more stock than is required for this recipe, but is a minimum workable amount to make

For the apricot purée
550g halved apricots
400ml apricot stock (see above)
To finish:
450g poached apricot purée
200ml cooking liquor
gellan gum
salt, to taste

Sheep's milk ice cream
(for 1 Pacojet canister)
25g caster sugar
1.3g sorbet neutral emulsifier/stabilizer
150g sheep's milk
75g sheep's yogurt
150ml water
30g milk powder
70g dextrose
35g trimoline

Honeycomb
80g caster sugar
12.5g honey
31g glucose
15ml water
3.5g bicarbonate of soda (baking soda), sifted

Roasted milk skins
1 litre full-fat (whole) milk
50g cream mixed with 25g full-fat (whole) milk
icing (confectioners') sugar, to dust →

For the apricot stock

Combine all the ingredients for the stock, including the apricot kernels, in a saucepan and bring to 105°C (121°F). Leave to cool and pour off 400ml of the stock and reserve to make the purée. Break up the apricot into the remaining stock and reserve, refrigerated, until ready to assemble the dish.

For the apricot purée

Combine the apricots and apricot stock in a saucepan and gently simmer for around 15 minutes until the fruit is cooked. Strain the fruit and reserve the stock. Purée the fruit in a food processor. Once the puréed fruit and stock have cooled, combine them with the gellan gum to a ratio of 5g gellan gum per 1kg of purée-and-stock combination. Heat this mixture to 85°C (185°F). Leave to cool and harden for at least 3 hours, then process it to a thick purée. Add a little salt if required. Reserve, refrigerated.

For the sheep's milk ice cream

To achieve ice cream of the correct texture, it's important to ensure each ingredient is added to the ice cream base when it reaches the stipulated temperatures.

Take 10 per cent of the caster sugar, combine it with the neutral stabilizer and set aside.

In a wide-based saucepan, combine the milk, yogurt and water and whisk so they are combined. Gently heat the mixture to 25°C (77°F) and add the milk powder, stirring constantly so that it doesn't fall to the bottom of the pan. Continue warming the mixture to 35°C (95°F) and add the remaining caster sugar, dextrose and trimoline. Continue to heat the mixture to 40°C (104°F), then add the neutral stabilizer/sugar mix. Continue to heat the ice cream base gently, whilst stirring constantly, until it reaches 85°C (185°F). Then remove the saucepan from the heat and emulsify the ice cream base with a stick blender. Place the finished base in a container and refrigerate or for at least 12 hours.

The following day, re-emulsify the mixture, then strain it through a fine chinois. Transfer it to a Pacojet canister and freeze to −28°C (−18°F). Pacotize and re-freeze at least twice before serving.

For the honeycomb

Combine the sugar, honey, glucose and water in a saucepan and bring the mixture to 153°C (307°F). Remove the pan from the heat and whisk in the bicarbonate of soda (baking soda). The mix will bubble rapidly. Pour onto a Silpat and allow to cool and harden.

Reserve some of the honeycomb as larger pieces for serving, then place the remaining honeycomb into a vacuum pack and seal lightly before smashing it up with a rolling pin or similar into a rough powder. Store in an airtight container in the freezer.

For the roasted milk skins

Preheat the oven (low fan) to 110°C (230°F). Put the milk into a wide-based rectangular pan (hotel pan) and leave in the oven for 1½ hours. The milk will form a skin. Remove the tray from the oven, taking care not to break the skin, and cover it with a sheet of greaseproof (wax) paper that has been brushed with the milk-and-cream mixture. Once the skin is stuck to the paper, lift the paper carefully to remove the milk skin from the surface of the milk. Place another sheet of paper on top and leave the skin to cool and harden. Freeze the milk skin.

Preheat the oven to 140°C (285°F). Once the milk skin is frozen, remove the papers and place the milk skin onto a Silpat-lined baking tray.

Roast the skin for around 6 minutes, until crisp but not darkly coloured. Remove from the oven and leave to cool, then dust the milk skin sheet with icing (confectioners') sugar. Break down the milk skin into pieces no larger than 1.5cm across. Keep in an airtight container. The roasted milk skins should be used soon after making. →

Milk crumble
50g clarified butter
125g skimmed milk powder
40g roasted milk skins
(see page 226)
40g toasted milk powder
6g cured egg yolk
9g honeycomb powder

For the milk crumble

Warm the clarified butter in a wide-based saucepan over a low heat. Once it is hot, just before smoking point, slowly sift in the milk powder, stirring quickly and constantly so that it does not catch or burn. As soon as the powder is completely hydrated, remove the pan from the heat and leave the milk crumb to cool.

Once cold, combine the crumb with the other ingredients, transfer to a sealed container and reserve in the freezer until needed. This crumble can over-hydrate at room temperature and become soggy and unpleasant on the palate, so it's best to keep it frozen.

To serve

Place a large dessertspoonful of the milk crumble on each serving plate. Around the outside of this, arrange 1 dessertspoonful of apricot stock, including some of the apricot pieces reserved in the stock. Add a few of the larger pieces of honeycomb. Cover 1 side of the milk crumble with a dessertspoonful of apricot purée, then add a quenelle of ice cream next to it and serve.

Sweet tomato and sweet ricotta

For 4 people

Ricotta
1 litre bio-dynamic cow's milk
30ml white vinegar

Tomato stock syrup
250ml water
250ml tomato water
  (see page 210)
335g caster sugar
100g crushed extra-ripe tomatoes
35 fennel seeds
5g Java long pepper
5g Jamaican pepper
50 coriander seeds
10 marigold leaves

Tomatoes
24 small-ish tomatoes of varying
  size, colour and variety

Honeycomb
80g caster sugar
12.5g honey
31g glucose
15ml water
3.5g bicarbonate of soda
  (baking soda), sifted

Hazelnuts
12 hazelnuts, shaved

Leaves and flowers
finely sliced marigold leaves
petals of perennial marigold

For the ricotta
Warm the milk to 80°C (176°F), then add
the vinegar and gently stir while increasing
the heat to 85°C (185°F). Allow the curds
to separate. Remove the milk from the heat
and allow it to cool to room temperature.
Strain the whey from the curds, transfer
the curds to ricotta baskets and leave to
harden for a couple of hours. Reserve the
whey for other dishes.

For the tomato stock syrup
Combine the water, tomato water, sugar
and tomatoes in a saucepan and bring to
the boil. Add the spices and marigold
leaves, remove from the heat and leave
to cool to room temperature.

For the tomatoes
Blanch and peel the tomatoes, then confit
them slowly in gently simmering tomato
stock syrup for 30 minutes. Leave to cool
in the syrup.

For the honeycomb
Follow the instructions on page 232
to prepare the honeycomb.

To finish
Place 2 tablespoons ricotta in the base
of each serving bowl and cover it with
tomatoes and some syrup to sweeten
the ricotta. Cover with a large spoonful
of honeycomb, the shaved hazelnuts,
some sliced marigold leaf and a scattering
of the petals.

Jostaberries with blackberry juice and eucalyptus, malted buckwheat ice

For 4 people

Malted buckwheat
Start the fermentation 3 months
   in advance
650g buckwheat
1.45 litres water
60g salt
30ml oil for every 100g of
   fermented buckwheat
   (dried of liquid)

Eucalyptus infusion
500ml water
100g caster sugar
seeds from 1 vanilla pod
5 black peppercorns, cracked
12g soft and vibrant eucalyptus
   leaves (such as those from
   lemon-scented gum)

Blackberry and eucalyptus juice
150ml raw blackberry juice
60ml eucalyptus infusion
salt, to taste

Jostaberries
10–15 jostaberries per serve,
   depending on their size

Malted buckwheat ice
(for 1 Pacojet canister)
25g caster sugar
1.3g sorbet neutral emulsifier/
   stabilizer
150g sheep's milk
75g sheep's yogurt
150ml water
30g milk powder
70g dextrose
35g trimoline
80g malted buckwheat

Honeycomb
80g caster sugar
12.5g honey
31g glucose
15ml water
3.5g bicarbonate of soda
   (baking soda), sifted

Milk crumble
50g clarified butter
125g skimmed milk powder

Roasted milk skins
1 litre full-fat (whole) milk
50ml cream mixed with 25ml
full-fat (whole) milk
icing (confectioners') sugar, to dust

Milk crunch
40g roasted milk skins
40g toasted milk powder
6g cured egg yolk
9g honeycomb powder

For the malted buckwheat
Combine the raw buckwheat, water and salt in a fermenting jar and leave in a cool, dark place for at least 3 months.

After the fermenting time has elapsed, strain off the water and dry the buckwheat on absorbent paper or kitchen towels, then toast it in a pan in the hot oil. When the buckwheat is a dark toasted colour, remove it from the pan onto absorbent paper to drain excess oil.

For the eucalyptus infusion
Combine the water, sugar, vanilla seeds and pepper in a saucepan. Bring to the boil, then pour it over the eucalyptus leaves, sealing the infusion quickly. Leave to stand at room temperature for approximately 20 minutes. Once the mixture is infused to your taste, strain off the leaves and chill the infusion.

For the blackberry and eucalyptus juice
Juice enough sun-ripened blackberries to produce 150ml juice. For a good yield it's worth juicing the pulp a second time. Combine the strained juice with eucalyptus syrup and season with a little salt. Keep covered and refrigerated until needed.

For the jostaberries
Pick the largest jostaberries that are deepest in colour just before they will be heated with the blackberry and eucalyptus juice – and don't refrigerate them.

Heat the blackberry and eucalyptus juice to just below boiling point, then pour it over the jostaberries. Leave them to cool to room temperature.

For the malted buckwheat ice
To achieve ice of the correct texture, it's important to ensure each ingredient is added to the base when it reaches the stipulated temperatures.

Take 10 per cent of the caster sugar, combine it with the neutral stabilizer and set aside.

In a wide-based saucepan, combine the milk, yogurt and water and whisk so they are combined. Gently heat the mix to 25°C (77°F) and add the milk powder, stirring constantly so that it doesn't fall to the bottom of the pan. Continue warming the

mixture to 35°C (95°F) and add the remaining caster sugar, the dextrose and trimoline. Continue to heat the mixture to 40°C (104°F), then add the neutral stabilizer/sugar mix. Continue to heat the ice cream base gently, whilst stirring constantly, until it reaches a temperature of 85°C (185°F). Then remove the saucepan from the heat, add the malted buckwheat and emulsify with a stick blender. Place the finished base in a container and refrigerate for at least 18 hours.

Once infused, strain the base through a fine sieve (strainer), removing any larger pieces of buckwheat, then re-emulsify the mixture, place it into a Pacojet canister and freeze it to minus −28°C (-18°F). Pacotize and churn this ice at least twice before serving.

For the honeycomb
Combine the sugar, honey, glucose and water in a saucepan and bring the mixture to 153°C (307°F). Remove the pan from the heat and whisk in the bicarbonate of soda (baking soda). The mix will bubble rapidly. Pour onto a Silpat and allow to cool and harden.

Place the honeycomb into a vacuum pack and seal lightly before smashing it up with a rolling pin or similar into a rough powder. Store in an airtight container in the freezer.

For the milk crumble
Follow the instructions on page 228 to make the milk crumble.

For the roasted milk skins
Follow the instructions on page 226 to make the roasted milk skins.

For the milk crunch
Combine the ingredients and keep in an airtight container in the freezer until needed.

To finish
Cover the base of each serving bowl with a little of the milk crunch. Divide the jostaberries into 4 portions and place one of these and a little of the blackberry and eucaplyptus liquor to one side of the bowl, then finish with a scoop of malted buckwheat ice.

Plums simmered with onions, honey and cultured milk

For 4 people

Plums
4 yellow-fleshed plums, such
  as Santa Rosa
100g caster sugar
300ml water
2 star anise

Onion stock
2kg large brown onions
olive oil
egg white
xanthan gum
salt, to taste

Honeycomb
80g caster sugar
12.5g honey
31g glucose
15ml water
3.5g bicarbonate of soda
  (baking soda), sifted

Cultured milk ice cream
(for 1 Pacojet canister)
25g caster sugar
1.3g sorbet neutral emulsifier/
  stabilizer
225ml cultured milk
150ml water
30g milk powder
70g dextrose
35g trimoline →

For the plums

Blanch and peel the plums. Reserve the plum flesh. Combine the skins with the sugar, water and star anise in a saucepan and bring to a boil. Strain off the skins and star anise and chill the sugar syrup.

Cut the plums in half and remove and discard the stones. Combine the flesh with the plum syrup in a vacuum pack and seal tightly. Cook the plums at 60°C (140°F) for around 15 minutes, depending on their ripeness – the end result should be plums that are cooked but not broken down. Once cooked sufficiently, chill the plums. When chilled, use a small pastry cutter to cut them into rounds – allow 5 rounds per serve.

For the onion stock

Prepare a barbecue.

Slice the onions in half through the skins and across the core. Rub the flesh of the onions with a small amount of oil and place the onions, flesh-side down, on a plancha and cook until blackened. Once black, transfer the onions to a barbecue. Set them slightly above the heat and allow the water inside the onions to boil.

When the water begins to bubble out of the onions, transfer them to a stainless steel bowl and cover with clingfilm (plastic wrap). Leave them to steam.

Preheat the oven to 70°C (158°F).

Remove the cooled onions from the bowl and, with the back of a paring knife, remove all traces of carbon. This step is important as any blackness will result in a bitter stock. Remove the skins and put the cleaned onions in a stainless steel bowl, wrap the bowl tightly with clingfilm and transfer it to the oven. Bake for 12 hours, leaving the onions to steam slowly and their sugars to caramelize.

Once this time has elapsed, remove the onions from the oven and push them several times through a juicer, extracting as much juice as possible. Then pass the juice through a fine chinois.

Mix the egg white with the juice at a ratio of 100g egg white to 1 litre juice. Put the mixture into a vacuum pack sealed without vacuum.

Set a steam oven to 100°C (212°F). Transfer the vacuum pack to the steam oven and cook for around 2 hours. (Alternatively, you can place the sealed bag into a pan of boiling water and boil it hard for the same period of time – just ensure the pan does not boil dry.) The protein in the egg will set during this period and clarify the liquid. Once the albumen is set and patches of clear liquid appear, remove the liquid from the bag and strain it through a fine sieve (strainer). Thicken the stock with xanthan gum at a ratio of 4g xanthan gum per 1 litre liquid. Season to taste and store, refrigerated, until needed.

For the honeycomb

Follow the recipe on page 232 to make the honeycomb.

For the cultured milk ice cream

To achieve ice cream of the correct texture, it is important to ensure each ingredient is added to the ice cream base when it reaches the stipulated temperatures.

Take 10 per cent of the caster sugar, combine it with the neutral stabilizer and set aside.

In a wide-based saucepan, combine the milk and water and whisk so they are combined. Gently heat the mix to 25°C (77°F) and add the milk powder, stirring constantly so that it does not fall to the bottom of the pan. Continue warming the mixture to 35°C (95°F) and add the remaining caster sugar, dextrose and trimoline. Continue to heat the mixture to 40°C (104°F), then add the neutral stabilizer/sugar mix. Continue to heat the ice cream base gently, whilst stirring constantly, until it reaches a temperature of 85°C (185°F). Then remove the saucepan from the heat and emulsify the ice cream base with a stick blender. Place the finished base in a container and refrigerate or for at least 12 hours.

The following day, re-emulsify the mixture, strain it through a fine chinois and place it in a Pacojet canister. Freeze to −28°C (−18°F). Pacotize and re-freeze at least twice before serving. →

Lime zest confit
1 mandarin
1 lemon
1 orange
375g caster sugar
250ml water
rind of 1 lime, cut into 5cm strips

To serve
Pedro Ximénez fortified wine

For the lime confit

Place the whole citrus fruits in a saucepan and cover with water. Slowly bring the water to a boil and blanch the fruits to remove a little of the bitterness in the zest. Leave to simmer for 2–3 minutes, then remove the fruit from the heat and discard the blanching water.

Combine the sugar and water and the blanched fruit in a saucepan and slowly bring to a simmer over a low heat, allowing the syrup to climb to 105°C (221°F). Once this temperature is reached, remove the saucepan from the heat and leave the fruit to cool in the syrup.

Blanch the lime zest from cold 3 times to remove any bitterness and combine with sufficient citrus syrup to cover. Place the mixture in a saucepan over a low heat and leave to confit slowly over several hours. The final result should see the zest slightly candied, not brittle and not overly soft. Remove from the heat and reserve the zest in the syrup until needed.

To serve

Place 5 plum pieces in a circle on each serving plate, leaving slightly uneven gaps between each piece, then pour a little of the onion stock over the top and into the centre of the plate. Put a little honeycomb (about 10g – just enough to support the ice cream) in the centre of the plums, then a few drops of Pedro Ximénez. Place 2 strips of lime zest randomly over the plums and then a quenelle of the ice cream on top of the honeycomb.

Red fruits, lemon and lovage, wild cabbage and buckwheat

For 4 people

Fermented buckwheat crisp
2 litres water
1.1kg buckwheat
500ml water, at room temperature
60g salt
icing (confectioners') sugar, to dust

Citrus stock syrup
2 mandarins
2 lemons
750g caster sugar
500ml water
Note – these quantities yield more
stock than is required for this
recipe

Citrus and berries
4 segments of lemon
4 segments of grapefruit
good mix of blackberries,
  blueberries, boysenberries,
  currants and different types of
  strawberry – you need 3–4 of
  each per serve
citrus stock syrup (see above)

Lemon curd
60ml lemon juice
95g caster sugar
75g whole eggs
30g egg yolks
1g gold leaf gelatine (½ leaf),
  hydrated
65g cold unsalted butter, diced
salt, to taste

Blackberry juice
200g blackberries
20ml citrus stock syrup
  (see above)

Wild cabbage juice
200g wild cabbage
80g large French sorrel leaves
20g large nasturtium leaves
  and stems
1g ascorbic acid
salt, to taste

Lovage powder
200g lovage leaves →

For the fermented buckwheat crisp

Bring the water to the boil. Add the buckwheat and cook it at a rolling boil for 5 minutes. Drain off the water and chill the buckwheat rapidly.

Combine 1.35kg of the cooked buckwheat with the 500ml water and the salt and seal tightly in a sterilized fermenting jar. Leave the jar at room temperature for a minimum of 30 days.

Once fermented, remove the buckwheat from the liquor and blanch it in boiling water for 2 minutes. Strain and, while it is still warm, roll out 200g of the fermented, blanched buckwheat between sheets of baking paper to an even thickness of 5mm. Place the sheet of buckwheat in the freezer to harden.

Preheat the oven to 160°C (320°F).

Once the sheet of buckwheat has hardened, the baking paper can be easily removed. Peel away the paper and place the buckwheat on a Silpat mat. Bake for 15–20 minutes or until the buckwheat has crisped and is a dark golden colour.

Remove the buckwheat from the oven and then lightly dust it with icing (confectioners') sugar through a sieve (strainer) so that it is evenly distributed across the entire sheet. Caramelize the sugar with a blowtorch. For a completely caramelized, candied buckwheat crisp, caramelize the wafer 3 times, adding new sugar each time.

Break the buckwheat crisp into small shards and store for up to 1 day only in an airtight container.

For the citrus stock syrup

Follow the instructions on page 224 to make the citrus stock syrup.

For the citrus and berries

Prepare the citrus. Allow 1 lemon and 1 grapefruit segment per plate. Cut each of the segments of both the lemon and grapefruit, across the segment, into 3–4 pieces, depending on their sizes. Combine them in a container.

Now prepare the red fruits. Cut large berries, such as blackberries and larger blueberries and strawberries, in half. If using strawberries, keep them separate from the other red fruits. If you are using white strawberries, keep those separate too, but combine the other fruits in one container.

Bring enough citrus syrup to cover the fruits to the boil and pour it over the various fruits. Let the fruits cook a little in the hot syrup, and then leave them to cool in the syrup.

For the lemon curd

Combine the lemon juice, sugar and eggs in a saucepan and heat to 85°C (185°F), whisking constantly. Add the hydrated gelatine, then transfer to a stand mixer.

Whisk the mixture at a medium speed setting until the temperature drops to 45°C (113°F). Add the butter. Once it has been incorporated, increase the speed and keep whisking the curd until it cools to room temperature. Season with a little salt, transfer to a container, cover with a lid and reserve, refrigerated.

For the blackberry juice

Juice well-ripened blackberries several times to extract everything from the pulp. Squeeze the juice through a fine sieve (strainer). Pour 100ml blackberry juice into a container and add the stock syrup. Keep chilled.

For the wild cabbage juice

Wash all the leaves in abundant water, then pat them dry. Chop the sorrel down a little, removing any obviously coarse parts of the wild cabbage and sorrel stems, which can ruin small electric juicers. Place the ascorbic acid into the vessel that will catch the juice and juice the leaves over the top. Stir the ascorbic acid through and season with salt as necessary. Cover the juice and keep cold until needed.

For the lovage powder

Dry the lovage in a dehydrator at 35°C (95°F). When completely dry, process to a fine powder, sifting away any bits of stem or pieces that were not dried correctly. Store in an airtight container. →

Blackberry and beetroot ice
(makes 2 Pacojet canisters)
90g caster sugar
800g blackberry juice
250ml beetroot (beet) juice
215g cocoa butter
175g dark chocolate with 70 per
  cent cocoa solids
195ml cream
2g salt

To finish
6–8 wild sorrel or wood sorrel
leaves, per serve

For the blackberry and beetroot ice

Stir the sugar into the juices until dissolved.

Melt the cocoa butter and chocolate together, then combine all the ingredients in a saucepan and gently heat to 35°C (95°F). Maintain this temperature, whilst emulsifying the mixture with a stick blender, for several minutes.

Pour the mix into Pacojet canisters and freeze rapidly. It is necessary that the mixture becomes rock hard and reaches a temperature below −30°C (−22°F).

Once frozen, shave the ice, 1 portion at a time, with the Pacojet, scooping off the fluffy ice that forms. Reserve the ice in a separate container in the freezer for service. The ice should be very fine and not clumped together.

To finish

Place a tablespoonful of the lemon curd in the centre of each serving plate, then drizzle both the blackberry and cabbage juices around the outside. On top of the curd, spoon over a good mixture of berries and citrus, then place some pieces of the buckwheat crisps and wood sorrel over and around the citrus. Dust with the lovage powder, then cover everything with the shaved blackberry and beetroot ice.

Parsnip and apple

I don't really know how this dish happened, but it's still around – and some people, it seems, come to the restaurant just to eat it, asking as every plate is placed before them, 'Is this the parsnip?' Or when it lands, after being in the dining room for a couple of hours, saying, 'Finally! I only came here for this'.

I started using parsnips before I opened Brae. It was while first baking and then frying different starch-based vegetable skins with varying results and for different uses that I fried a parsnip skin and then shaped it back, as much as possible, into its original shape. It was served with blueberries and crème fraîche at that time, upside down like a cannoli, with the open side facing up, and was just a vehicle, really, for carrying the blueberries – but it was delicious with the fruit and cream, like a really good pastry.

When it got down to the nitty-gritty of the dishes and menu for the opening of Brae, I decided I wanted to use the parsnip but to turn it upside down – really, as a gesture to myself and Damien, my sous chef, a sign that we were about to turn everything on its head. It was one of those processes where, in my head, I could see this beautiful, immaculate golden cone shape covering a mousse of apple and parsnip, like it was perfectly stuffed back in and sitting on the plate and, because it seemed so vivid and clear in my mind, I didn't really give it any time.

Before the opening, and once the kitchen and renovation was nearly completed, Damien started working on all the dish ideas I'd been getting together for six months or so. Together, we developed ideas for several weeks and came up with what we thought would be a solid opener and something the staff could handle while we found our feet. The rest of the kitchen team and the front of house started about one week before the opening, but mainly did gardening and cleaning jobs, so everything would be right for the opening, while Damien and I plugged away at the menu. We had a soft opening planned for about twenty friends and family the day before we opened to the public – and the night before that, Damien and I cooked the first menu we would serve for the staff, so they could taste it, so beverage pairings could be confirmed, and so we could have a run-through ourselves. The parsnip was written in as the last dessert.

To be completely honest, I can't even remember what the first version of this dessert was but, for that dinner, the practice run for the practice run, I tried to plate one and decided it was too disgusting to serve to the staff, and so it was left, un-plated and unserved.

I left that night knowing that we were a dish short for the menu and our real opening to the public in two days' time, which was already booked out.

I think sometimes, in a creative sense, with a bit of pressure, it's like you're backed into a corner, and you can just get lucky. I went home and basically went over and over on paper and in my mind all the possibilities I could imagine for a dish with these two core ingredients, drawing diagram after diagram of plate-ups and thinking about various nuances of the same ingredients that make that dish. I pretty much stayed up all night.

In the morning, we started very early, and first on my agenda was sorting out the parsnip. I made a fresh mousse with the apple and parsnip purée, but really mounted it this time with loads of shaved freeze-dried apple, which gave it the lift that was missing. Then a chamomile caramel was made, which goes so well with apple, and more freeze-dried apple pieces were chopped, to be added as flavour and texture to the plate. The original idea in my mind of what this thing should be had stopped me seeing what it could be, and had basically arrested both the creative process and the important trial-and-error process in their tracks. When I plated the new parsnip it sat so nicely over the mousse and I was so disappointed that I had not been more open-minded in exploring the possibilities that I Microplaned freeze-dried apple all over it and the plate.

That's how that dish has remained. We've improved the frying and shaping but, unfortunately, we can never improve on the time it takes to bake and clean the parsnips at this stage — it's one of the most simple but tedious two-ingredient dishes on our menu. But it still remains, and although many people love it, I must say I'm tiring a little of it, but leave it on the menu almost as a reminder to be more open-minded to possibilities, to maintain focus during the creative process and see them through.

Parsnip and apple

For 4 people

Parsnip
2 large parsnips
sunflower oil, for deep-frying

Apple and parsnip mousse
75ml cream
½ sheet (1g) gold leaf gelatine
36g caster sugar
24ml water
2 egg yolks
20g apple purée
12.5g parsnip purée
4g freeze-dried apple powder
salt, to taste

Apple and chamomile infusion
450ml filtered water
12g dried chamomile flowers
50g caster sugar
4 Granny Smith apples, peeled

Apple caramel
50g caster sugar
450ml apple and chamomile
    infusion (see above)

To serve
5 freeze-dried apple quarters
    (3 cut into 12 pieces and 2
    quarters left whole for grating)

For the parsnip

Preheat the oven to 140°C (285°F).

Wrap the parsnips in kitchen (aluminum) foil and bake for 3 hours. Once cool, cut through the skin on 1 side of each parsnip, then remove the core and all the flesh, ensuring the skin remains intact as one piece. Carefully scrape any remains of the flesh from the skin. Discard the core and flesh. Slice each skin lengthways so that there are 2 equal halves (4 in total) and leave the skins to dry a little.

Once semi-dried, fry the skins at 165°C (330°F) until a golden 'pastry' colour is achieved. While the skins are still hot, shape them into their original cone shape and place on absorbent paper to cool. The finished crisp skins will appear as though they have been hollowed out. Keep in a cool, dry place until needed in service.

For the apple and parsnip mousse

In a stand mixer, whisk the cream to soft peaks. Reserve in a cool place.

Soak the gelatine in cold water and, once hydrated, remove it, squeezing out the excess moisture. Put it to the side.

Combine the sugar and water in a saucepan and place it over a medium heat. While the sugar syrup is warming, put the egg yolks into the stand mixer and begin to beat on a medium speed. Heat the syrup to 120°C (248°F), turn off the heat and add the reserved gelatine. Once the gelatine is dissolved, reduce the stand mixer speed slightly and drizzle the sugar syrup between the beater and the side of the bowl to mix it with the egg yolk, taking care not to hit the beaters. Once all the sugar syrup is incorporated, increase the speed setting to maximum and beat the eggs until they are shiny, have increased 6–8 times in volume, have cooled to room temperature and are almost white. Placing a bowl of iced water underneath the mixing bowl will help to bring the temperature of meringue down quickly.

Fold in the apple and parsnip purées and freeze-dried apple powder, and a little of the whipped cream. When combined well, fold in the rest of the cream until the mixture is homogenous. Place the mousse into a piping (pastry) bag and reserve, refrigerated, until needed.

For the apple and chamomile infusion

Bring the water to the boil and pour it over the chamomile. Cover immediately and leave to infuse for 6 minutes. Strain and discard the chamomile and combine the infusion with the sugar and apples.

Place the ingredients in a vacuum pack and seal on maximum pressure. Cook at 82°C (180°F) for 90 minutes. Strain and discard the apples. Season with salt and chill the infusion immediately. Store, covered and refrigerated, until required.

For the apple caramel

Caramelize the sugar in a wide-based pan, taking it to a deep, dark golden colour. Deglaze with the apple and chamomile infusion and let reduce to a thick caramel. Store, covered, at room temperature.

To serve

In the centre of each flat serving plate, pipe around 10cm of mousse in a straight line and drizzle the caramel over and around the mousse. Place 4 pieces of freeze-dried apple around the mousse and then lay a piece of parsnip skin over the top so that the mousse is hidden underneath. Using a Microplane, grate one-half of a piece of freeze-dried apple over the parsnip and serve.

Kitchen Dos and Don'ts

Kitchen Dos and Don'ts

Kitchen Dos and Dont's

Kitchen Dos and Don'ts

Please...
– do wash before you arrive at work in the morning, don't arrive after a big weekend looking shipwrecked, do eat breakfast before you arrive and drink plenty of
water throughout the day, do arrive before the start time, do greet others in the
morning, do wear a mild deodorant if you are prone to body odour – especially
on the big days, do arrive looking like you're a professional, do wear clean/ironed
whites, don't turn up with a jacket with a big rip in it, don't wear the same trousers
all week – especially those ones with the hole in the knee, do clean your finger-
nails – especially after cleaning fish or meat or digging in the garden, do keep
your kitchen shoes clean, do clean your knives – often, do sharpen your knives –
often, don't wipe your dirty hands on your apron or your arse, do wash your hands
with soap and dry them regularly throughout the day, don't walk around with two
tea towels like you're wearing a grass skirt, don't use the same tea towel all day,
don't grab a tea towel with a massive hole in it and think that looks good I'll use
that today, do throw out that tea towel with a massive hole or burn in it, don't
taste things or eat your lunch off your spatula or tweezers, don't taste things and
then put that spoon straight back into the thing you just tasted without first rinsing
or washing it or dipping it in the hot water your spoons are sitting in – even in
service, don't ask me to taste something and offer it to me on a dirty spoon, do
change your spoon water regularly and keep it hot, don't ask me to taste something
that we serve hot but give it to me fridge-cold, don't ask me to taste something
you have not tasted yourself, don't carry your own 'tasting spoon' in your back
pocket – there is only one type of spoon in the kitchen for tasting and plating and
we all use the same ones, do taste things I've given back to you seasoned and lock
in that flavour for next time, do smell things as well as taste them, do write recipes
down the first time, do date the recipe and record who gave it to you, don't change
that recipe unless I or the sous chef ask you to change it, do weigh things correctly,
do use a calculator to work out any amount changes to recipes, don't let timers
ring without turning them off immediately, don't turn someone's timer off and not
tell them, don't walk through the kitchen and not notice things, don't walk past
something on the floor and not pick it up, don't work like a maniac and chop stuff
all onto the floor, do put all your appropriate green scraps into the chicken feed
bucket, do put all your other green scraps into the compostables bin, don't put
some ridiculous item of half-prepped food onto the family meal shelf in a container
like it's a really big help and label it 'staff', do occasionally, when it's your turn, cook
a really fucking good meal for everyone that helps to get the spirits up in the
middle of a really busy week, don't stand at the stove working and not notice a pot
come to the boil or something burning right next to you, don't walk past a boiling
stock and not turn it down or let its owner know, do feel free to skim something
you notice needs to be skimmed, do write a detailed and easy-to-understand and
concise prep list for each day/service, don't continually study that prep list without
actually doing the work that's on that prep list, do not work all morning with a

prep list on your bench – try and actually remember what jobs you will do next, do discuss the day's plan with your section, do give more than one job to those in your section so they get the full picture of the day and don't think one job is all they need to do, do work to agreed times, do set a timer for jobs to see how long they take, do try and beat that time next time, do be reasonable when giving others a time to complete tasks, don't eat family meals in your section while you are working – that includes both meal times, do stop to eat family meals, do have meals with everyone else, don't have a half-finished cold coffee in your section in your way and knock it but don't then finish it and don't clean up the spilled coffee, do keep drinking lots of water even when it's cold, do have damp folded cloths on the edge of the bench in your section, do only have cloths that you need, don't have a big stack of cloths for no reason, don't stash a big stack of damp cloths in your fridge and let them go musty before using them, do use the cloths to wipe up continually, do rinse them out and wring them out before folding them every time and returning them to the same spot perfectly folded, do put a cloth in the washing basket when it needs it, don't stash trays or other equipment in your fridge, not letting others use it because you will need it in 5 hours at service time, don't use a tap or sink without wiping it dry when you are finished, don't constantly use the sink in someone else's section and always wet their mise en place, don't rummage around in someone else's fridge or section looking for something – ask them if you need something they may have, do ask politely, do give things to others if they need it, do give someone a piece of equipment they may need even if you were planning on using it later after you finish what you are currently doing, do scrub your board down before dumping it in the wash-up, don't put burnt pots in the wash up – wash them yourself, don't put hot things in stupid places, do let everyone know when something is hot in a stupid place, do stack things from largest to smallest in the wash-up, do not leave containers in the wash-up still labelled – you know you're getting 10 push-ups for that! Do place trays gently to keep the noise down, do keep the noise down including voices, don't smash stainless steel objects into each other, do put things through the dishwasher to help out, do put things back on the shelves for the kitchen hands when they need it, do remember the dinner-ware is handmade, do treat items and the work space with respect, do try not to break things, let me or the sous chef know when you do break things, do close the walk-in door both on the way in and way out, do put things in the right places in the walk-in, don't eat food in the walk-in, don't break holes in film so you can eat something in the walk-in, don't spill something in the walk-in and not wipe it up, don't put something in the walk-in that is not covered and labelled, label containers and bags correctly in writing everyone can read and on tape that has been cut not torn, and don't label in some code that no-one else knows, do not put open vac bags in the walk-in, do not put hot stocks into the walk-in, do cool everything down quickly via the blast chiller, don't open a fridge drawer in your section and leave it open while you look at something on your bench, do not open an oven door and walk away leaving it open, do try to listen to the commands from the pass in service, do show you're paying attention and answer yes even when the command is not for you, do inform the chef de partie who controls the next dish on the menu when you have sent the dish before, do try to read the service and stay ahead of what may happen next, do try and have things ready when they are called away, not starting them when they are called away, do help out others who are going down in the service, do bring things up to the pass in an order that facilitates the smooth flow of the service, do clean up relentlessly in service, do keep your section in a manner that would suggest you are fucking crushing it not going down, do give clear instructions to commis and stagiaires and anyone plating about what's coming up to the pass and in what order, do speak in a controlled manner to each other in service, do speak in a formal manner in service so that nothing is left to chance or misinterpreted, do enjoy yourself in service and let it show – yes, chef, do push on chef, do clean down like a machine and leave your fridge looking like the best version of an upmarket deli or stall, do greet our guests when they enter the kitchen with a smile and a friendly hello – please also say goodbye and goodnight to the guests when they leave the kitchen, do keep working completely focused, even when a table of super-VIPs enter the kitchen and start asking you questions or watching you plate up a dish, do keep doing service but work around customers who are in the kitchen so that they feel at home and not in the way, do cook really beautiful food, do have and continually develop skills, do improve, do try and be better all the time, do enjoy repetition, do enjoy detailed, difficult work, do try to understand the work that goes into the garden and don't trash it while you are picking in the morning, looking for that VIP portion, do take time on a closed day to walk around the property with a different perspective and become familiar with where everything is in the different gardens, do eat food on your day off, do cook food on your day off for friends and really enjoy the act of cooking for another who's important to you, do get drunk, do get high occasionally and let loose, do listen to music, do go to galleries or other creative spaces and enjoy other creative work, do go to other restaurants, don't go to restaurants just to criticise, do try to not always critique other chefs but just enjoy the differences out there.

Index

This book is deciated to Jules and Ivy, and to Simon, Damien and the entire Brae family, past and present. We could never do what we do without your belief and dedication. Finally, thanks to Colin Page for his brilliant photography.

The publishers would like to thank Vanessa Bird, Jodie Gaudet, and Salima Hirani for their contributions to the book.

Recipe notes:
Some of the recipes require advanced techniques, specialist equipment and professional experience to achieve good results.

Exercise a high level of caution when following recipes involving any potential hazardous activity, including the use of high temperatures, open flames and when deep-frying. In particular, when deep-frying, add food carefully to avoid splashing, wear long sleeves and never leave the pan unattended.

Cooking times are for guidance only, as individual ovens vary. If using a fan (convection) oven, follow the manufacturer's instructions concerning oven temperatures.

Some recipes include raw or very lightly cooked eggs, meat, or fish and fermented products. These should be avoided by the elderly, infants, pregnant women, convalescents and anyone with an impaired immune system.

Exercise caution when making fermented products, ensuring all equipment is spotlessly clean, and seek expert advice if in any doubt.

When no quantity is specified, for example of oils, salts, and herbs used for finishing dishes or for deep-frying, quantities are discretionary and flexible.

All herbs, shoots, flowers and leaves should be picked fresh from a clean source. Exercise caution when foraging for ingredients; any foraged ingredients should only be eaten if an expert has deemed them safe to eat.

Phaidon Press Limited
Regent's Wharf
All Saints Street
London N1 9PA

Phaidon Press Inc.
65 Bleecker Street
New York, NY 10012

phaidon.com

First published 2017
© 2017 Phaidon Press Limited

ISBN 978 0 7148 7414 2

A CIP catalogue record for this book is available from the British Library and the Library of Congress.

Commissioning Editor: Ellie Smith
Project Editor: Eve O'Sullivan
Production Controller: Amanda Mackie
Photography: Colin Page
Design: Hubert & Fischer

Printed in China